Then & **Now**

LYMINGTON

AND PENNINGTON

The brewer's horse-drawn dray cart offloads beer barrels in St Thomas' Street at the Six Bells Inn, named after the church tower. This hostelry provided the beer for the town's peace celebrations in 1814. Next door was the Dorset Arms pub.

Then & Now
LYMINGTON
AND PENNINGTON

COMPILED BY Brian J. Down

TEMPUS

For 700 years Lymington was a principal manufacturer and exporter of sea salt, with trading ships of up to 1,300 tons displacement berthing at the Town Quay, able to work the double tides within the deep river. That situation dramatically changed in 1731 when a Boldre merchant captain, William Cross, took it upon himself to dam the river and exact a toll on all who crossed over. Ships also carried Walhampton bricks to the West Country. Fishing was always an important trade, with Lymington fishermen venturing out into the Solent. To afford them better use of time, their wives would row out in punts and tie their menfolk's food and drink in a basket on the last stake in the river. The drink was contained in 'black jack' tarred-leather flasks. This strategic river marker continues to be known as 'Jack in the Basket'.

ACKNOWLEDGEMENTS

This book is dedicated to my wife Kath, in recognition of her foregoing any thoughts of a normal retirement.

I am also indebted to the kind folk who have supplemented my own collection of old photographs, principally Geoff and Mavis Isted, Alby Doe, Ron Jennings, and Steve Marshall, Curator of the St Barbe Museum.

First published 2003

Tempus Publishing Limited
The Mill, Brimscombe Port,
Stroud, Gloucestershire, GL5 2QG

© Brian J. Down, 2003

The right of Brian J. Down to be identified as the Author of this work has been asserted in accordance with the Copyrights, Designs and Patents Act 1988.

British Library Cataloguing in Publication Data.
A catalogue record for this book is available from the British Library.

ISBN 0 7524 2956 6

Typesetting and origination by Tempus Publishing Limited
Printed in Great Britain by Midway Colour Print, Wiltshire

CONTENTS

INTRODUCTION

Idyllically situated on the shores of the Solent, surrounded to the north by the ancient New Forest created by William the Conqueror in 1074 as a royal hunting ground, the area which includes Lymington dates back to Buckland Rings and its time as a busy trading port for the Celts in the Iron Age. These Ancient Britons constructed an early defensive earthwork at Ampress, and later, possibly after 500 BC, the seven-acre Buckland Rings hill fort, captured by Vespasian in AD 43, which still survives in a good state of preservation. In 1744, 200lb of Roman coins were unearthed near there. By the time of William I's Domesday Book of 1086, Lymington was referred to as 'Lentune'. Lymington has no Charter from the Crown, for William de Redvers, 5th Earl of Devon, realising the opportunity to make a profit from a market and fair, granted his Charter of privileges between 1193 and 1217, which created a planned pegged-out Borough of New Lymington within the bounds of the original manor of Lentune. The Charter was extended by Earl Baldwin de Redvers around 1256. The 1270 Charter of Isabella de Fortibus led to burgesses themselves electing reeves, known as mayors, by 1413: the first known reeve (*prepositus*) in the Borough of New Lymington was Roger de Insula in 1270, and the first known reeve of Old Lymington was Roger Hosebond, 1270. The width of some burgage plots in the New Borough are one rod, pole or perch wide ($16\frac{1}{2}$ feet); Stanwell House is exactly four rods, Pilgrims exactly three, all within $\frac{1}{2}$ inch – so originally they probably represented that number of properties.

The wide Lymington River was for years navigable beyond Ampress, kept free of silt thanks to the scouring action of the double tides, until, in 1731, the merchant captain William Cross built a dam which later became a toll bridge – and despite an outcry by the local Corporation and pedestrians, the Council lost a court case at Winchester alleging the Captain's trespass, so the river inevitably silted up. By the fourteenth century the town was prospering from manufacturing salt and importing wine, but went on to be noted for its seventeenth and eighteenth-century smuggling activities along the Pennington foreshore, with spirits, silks and spices being the favourite commodities, causing Daniel Defoe to declare when visiting the town around 1727: 'I do not find they have any foreign commerce except it be what we call smuggling…' Brandy-kegs were buried in the river mud whenever the alarm was raised, before being recovered in carts with false platforms; good use was also made of several drainage tunnels around the Quay area. During Edward III's reign, in 1345, Lymington provided nine ships and 159 men for the invasion of France – almost double Portsmouth's contribution. At one time there were forty-five inns and ale houses scattered around the town.

Lymington had become a port of some considerable significance, for the town became a principal manufacturer of fine quality salt for over 700 years. Salt was an important and valuable commodity not only for culinary purposes, but also for curing skins, preparing leather, and using as a flux to solder pipes and gutters. A line of 163 salt pans extended along the coastline between Pylewell on the eastern side of Lymington River and Keyhaven to the west, each producing around three tons of salt per week and burning nineteen bushels of coal per ton – so that at one time the town imported more coal than London, shipped in from Newcastle and Sunderland. The sea water was drawn into ponds, and allowed to partially evaporate, leaving a briny liquor. Twelve-foot-high wind pumps elevated this brine into cisterns on stilts, before being filtered into metal pans inside brick boiling houses, leaving evaporated salt deposits.

Besides home consumption, during the nineteen years from 1724 to 1743 no less than 4,612 tons was exported from Lymington in sixty-four ships to America, Newfoundland, Holland, the Baltic, Ireland and the Channel Islands. This busy trade led to £55,000 of taxes reaching the Exchequer in 1755, and forty-nine years later annual production reached 6,000 tons. The weekly boiling lasted continuously from Sunday midnight to eight o'clock Saturdays, with operations based on the summer weather – an exceptional season being twenty-two weeks, an average of around sixteen, though in 1802 merely two weeks owing to volcanic eruptions around the world. But in 1808 there was local fury when punitive Government duty reached 15s per bushel, whereas the salt's actual value was just 1s. With railways able to transport mined Cheshire salt, and the crippling taxation, the salt trade ceased in Lymington by 1845.

Despite its comparatively small number of burgesses, Lymington returned two Members of Parliament from the reign of Queen Elizabeth I, the first representatives elected in 1584 being Anthony Cooke and Richard Cooke. A century later Lymington's loyalty to the Crown was questioned when Mayor Thomas Dore raised around a hundred local men to support the Duke of Monmouth, whom he joined at Sedgmoor. When the Duke lost that battle, Dore fled for his life and was fortunate to elude Judge Jefferies, was pardoned, and in 1689 became one of Lymington's MPs. In 1832 the constituency was extended to include parts of Pennington and Boldre. The 1867 Second Reform Act reduced the town's representation to one MP, until it lost all personal representation when forced to merge with the New Forest under the Redistribution of Seats Act of 1885. Following a short period when Lymington became a joint constituency with Christchurch, New Forest was divided into two, East and West, for the 1997 General Election.

Large numbers of French immigrants and Royalists, together with their families, landed at Lymington from the time of the French Revolutionary wars until the end of the Napoleonic wars, 1792 to 1815, so that they exceeded the local population of just over 2,378. The old Manor House and surrounding farmland at Buckland became the barracks for 600 French Royal Marines; the French Artillery was stationed in the Malthouse and nearby building in New Lane; while the refugee Corps of Loyal Emigrants were housed in Quadrille Court, St Thomas' Street. Many were later killed in the disastrous 1795 Quiberon Expedition, wounded survivors returning for treatment in the old Tithe Barn, which was demolished in the 1920s.

Detailed model of a Lymington saltworks.

Born in Penzance, Charles Curry was three years old when his father, editor of the *Cornish Telegraph*, died, so the Institute of Journalists met his boarding school fees. Emigrating to Canada in 1912, he became a journalist for the *Toronto Star*, but within two years he returned for First World War service with the Canadian Expeditionary Forces, posted to a tented camp on Salisbury Plain where he contracted pneumonia. His article expressing personal concern over injured Canadian troops in France being sent straight back to the Front Line without recuperation so impressed Beaverbrook that he was made editor of the *Canadian Daily Record*. Following victory in 1918, Charles joined Beaverbrook's *Daily Express*, but resigned on principle after staff were fired to appease shareholders, before being immediately re-employed. Accompanied by his wife, Charles was re-engaged on the *Toronto Star* until Canada's inhospitable climate led to their return. He became editor of the *Buckingham Advertiser*, before restarting the *Christchurch Times* in 1925, which had closed through a libel action. When that prospered once more, in 1932 he became a partner in the *New Milton Advertiser*, building a printing works on a New Milton plot and purchasing second-hand equipment. Charles struggled after his partner defaulted on the agreement, but in 1932 he founded the *Lymington Times*, occupying one-third of No. 39 St Thomas' Street shop front. He fought off fierce commercial opposition from the *Lymington Chronicle*, which eventually admitted defeat by offering its title for £100. During the Second World War all the staff, including his elder son Charles jnr, were called up for active service, so younger son Teddy left grammar school to operate a Linotype setting machine. Charles jnr took over as editor a few years before his father died in 1966, and the firm became the last in the country to modernise from hot-metal to di-litho, when purchasing and erecting the former Yorkshire Evening Post rotary press (pictured above). Teddy retired in 1997, though Charles jnr continues as editor, the circulation reaching a record 23,000 in 2002.

Thankfully apart from one or two exceptions, the distinctive façades of shops and houses along Lymington High Street have changed little over the years, most retaining their fine Georgian features. There have been a few major modifications to its highway. Originally, part of the churchyard stood on the southern side of St Thomas' church, until in 1821 the graves gave way to the widening of the passage along the High Street. Probably one of the first instances of 'pedestrianisation' came when sturdy metal railings were erected along the top of Quay Hill, thereby causing horse-drawn vehicles bound for the Quay to detour via South Street (now Captain's Row). Around 1905 the shop at the foot of town hill on its northern side, No. 139 High Street, was demolished in order to widen the highway for traffic at its junction with Gosport Street.

By the turn of the century horse-drawn transport around the town was beginning to give way to motorised vehicles, causing residents' horror owing to their speed, noise and fumes. The first

recorded car to be seen in Lymington was in September 1897, which belonged to the owner of Linden House in New Lane (now New Street). The following year motoring pioneer the Hon. John Scott Montagu, second Lord Montagu of Beaulieu, drove George Cornwallis-West of Milford at the startling speed of 25mph. Pennington residents had to wait until 1903 before one of its inhabitants owned a private car, which belonged to E. Powell King of Wainsford Road.

Lymington's first Town Hall was in a state of disrepair by 1300. Another was constructed in 1463, at Nos 30 and 31, on the south side of the High Street, courtesy of a Lymington widow who presented the town with a messuage and site. When that became obsolete, the next Town Hall was constructed in 1684 at Nos 93 and 94, on the opposite side of the street. This was succeeded in 1720 by a substantial four-storey building in the centre of the High Street between the top of Town Hill and the New Street junction, with a spacious meeting room on the first floor, where in 1789 George III visited Lymington and received the mayor and Corporation. Ultimately this structure was deemed an annoying obstruction to horse-drawn carriages and other vehicles, leading to its demolition in 1858.

In 1913 the fifth Town Hall was constructed on the northern side, midway up Town Hill, after the generous bequest of two houses, 117 and 118 High Street, by Mrs Martha Earley. When converting the houses was found to be impractical, Mrs Ellen Hewitt – Mrs Earley's sister – graciously offered to meet the cost of a new Town Hall on this site. She laid the foundation stone on 12 February 1913, and these offices continued to be occupied until councillors voted for a more modern building, on the allotments in Avenue Road, which the Queen formally opened in July 1966. This Town Hall took on less importance after Lymington Borough was swallowed by New Forest District Council on Local Government reorganisation in 1974.

The wedding took place at Holy Trinity Church, Dover, on 15 April 1873, of Ringwood draper George Elliott and housemaid Miss Elizabeth Decent. The honeymoon was brief, for within four days the couple, with just £225 between them, opened the Lymington Clothing Mart at No. 87 High Street, rented at £7 a quarter. Such was their success, with three pairs of trousers sold for 5s 11d, that in 1890 they moved to more spacious shop premises opposite, 44-46, aiming at a high-class clientele. Three years later their eldest son Edward joined the business at a £25 salary, the firm employing its own tailors and shoe repairers. By 1916 branches had been opened at Lyndhurst and New Milton, to be followed by Brockenhurst, Freshwater on the Isle of Wight, and Highcliffe. George died in 1928.

Edward's younger daughter Peggy ignored his Victorian views that she should not enter the family business – and indeed needed all her considerable skills after her father died in 1948, with the Church, Freemasons, and employees the beneficiaries of his will. Peggy and her husband John battled to survive, later joined by daughter Jenny and son-in-law Ulrich Welker, and now by grandson Neil, still running a highly successful family business in the town.

The Tiller family show patriotic fervour on the occasion of Queen Victoria's Silver Jubilee in 1862. On the right-hand side of the entrance to his business as nurseryman, florist and purveyor of fancy goods at Nos 8-9 High Street, stands George Tiller and his wife Isobel (Dolly), alongside their spinster daughters Bertha and Isobel who, along with brother Fred, ran a nursery garden around the corner in Gosport Street (now Trafalgar Place) upon their father's demise. No. 8 later became a newsagent's shop run by Mrs Ethel Dimmick, while No. 9 was rebuilt as Bale the hairdresser and High St East post office. Further down in the picture, at Nos 6 and 7, is the family grocery business of Michael Coughlan, later subdivided as 'Chappy' Bran's butchers shop and Rugg's the tobacconist (now gift and handyman shops). On the left, at No. 5, was the British & Colonial Meat Company. Mr C. Balls ran his radio shop at Nos 2-3, probably the oldest shop in Lymington, possibly built before 1690, with his son Elton Balls who later expanded the business into No. 5 and saw the arrival of television in the town.

To the right of the picture, past the billboard, lay No. 10, home of W. Smith the surgeon until, in 1851, it became the Albion Inn where the landlord W. Thring also acted as town crier, bill-poster and church vestry clerk. That building was demolished, and the site was an allotment until the Masonic Hall was erected there for the Powney and New Forest Lodges, the foundation stone being laid on 3 September 1926, by the Rt Hon. James Edward, 5th Earl of Malmesbury.

In 1797, John King began his Lymington solicitor's practice in the substantial house Brackens, previously owned by Obadiah Newell (in the centre of the lower picture) in South Street, now renamed Captain's Row. There he lived and worked as the sole practitioner until, in 1826, Edward Horatio Moore was admitted as a solicitor, five years later becoming a partner in the firm King & Moore. John King retired in 1836, and Edward Moore remained a partner for fifty-eight years until his death in 1889, by which time the practice operated from No. 15 High Street, known as Moore & Rawlins. The following year Mr Rawlins moved to No. 38 High Street, and George Octavius Vores was taken into the partnership. Subsequent partners included George Vicary, Alfred Trestrail, and in 1931 Cecil 'Purple' Blatch. By 1938, Cecil Blatch was the sole partner of Moore & Blatch, and whilst he served as a Squadron-Leader during the Second World War, managing clerk W. Bradshaw ran the firm virtually single-handed.

Following the hostilities Noel Cowper became a partner, and in 1951 the practice moved into their present elegant Georgian residence at No. 51 High Street (pictured) with its extensive gardens and views to the Isle of Wight. Oliver Ziegler was next to join the partnership, and by the time Cecil Blatch retired in 1970 he was president of the Union Internationale des Avocats. In 1957 the firm opened an office in Hythe, followed by others, principally Ringwood, Totton and Milford, before the Southampton practice of Brian Colenso was purchased in 1974, now under the Moore & Blatch umbrella.

'The Leading Hotel in Lymington' was the proud boast of the Angel Hotel, one of the oldest coaching inns in Lymington. Its earliest known date is 1675 and it was originally called The George. By the eighteenth century, the stagecoach era saw the Angel supplying sustenance for horses and passengers, while during the 1820s and '30s six different coaches operated to a regular timetable between Lymington and Southampton, and thence on to London (which took around twelve hours), Bristol and Brighton. Each carriage was named, with the 'Telegraph' operating out of the Angel yard. Passengers often loved to sit high up in front alongside coachman Jockey Beale, despite being open to the elements.

Backhurst & Sons, jobmasters, carriage and bus proprietors, ran their local service from the Angel Hotel Mews, advertising New Forest coaching excursions every Monday and Thursday during the summer months. Fred 'Tammy' Neal, pony-boy and boot-boy at the Angel, became the first to drive a motor bus around the town, a Stout made in Salisbury for Mr Backhurst. His buses and brakes ran daily, except Sundays, between Lymington and Milford (tel. Lymington 50), leaving at 10.40 a.m., and 12.33, 2.57, 4.47 and 7.19 p.m., arriving at Milford within thirty-five minutes. From the Angel Hotel's balcony all-important proclamations were declared by such eminences as the MP or mayor. At other times waiters and waitresses served genteel customers with afternoon teas, aloof of the High Street's hurly-burly below.

The Londesborough Hotel (on the left) was originally known as The Nag's Head. By 1828 three horse-drawn coaches left Lymington daily, bound for London, including the 'Independent' from The Nag's Head, and the 'Telegraph' from The Anchor & Hope (previously The Crown) at No. 96 High Street, reaching Southampton within $2\frac{1}{2}$ hours. Nag's Head Field, now Grove Gardens, was where coach and post-chaise horses were let out to graze, while the paddock was at the rear of The Angel Hotel (originally The George). When King William and Queen Mary were proclaimed at the Market Cross in 1687, The Nag's Head charged 30s for a hogshead of beer (a cask containing around fifty imperial gallons). Lord Londesborough, whilst staying in Lyndhurst, regularly quenched his thirst here, so the thrilled landlord deemed this such an honour that, in 1884, he tore down The Nag's Head sign, renaming the establishment after his celebrated customer. Extensive greenhouses and gardens to the rear provided fresh produce for the hotel's excellent cuisine.

Those grounds were acquired by the Hants & Dorset bus company for their Lymington depot. Such was the narrow access that bus drivers had inches to spare between The Londesborough and No. 35 High Street, once the London Central Meat Co., then Ashton Smith the florist, until that property was demolished in 1943 to provide a wider bus entrance. Leslie Ashton Smith moved his business to No. 51 High Street, previously the Waltham Arms pub.

father ran the Angel Hotel in Lymington High Street. Rowland continued to operate his Central Grocery Store as a typical old family business, with eight staff and an errand boy on a trade bike. His elder daughter Betty was responsible for the accounts, while his younger daughter Beryl first worked at Lloyd's Bank, then as a secretary with Wellworthy during the Second World War. Rowland once received a rebuke from the Vicar of Lymington for displaying toilet rolls in his shop window on a Sunday.

In the early 1930s he purchased his first van, later upgraded to a smart Bedford, delivering groceries to such outlying parts as Sway and Boldre. He smoked his own bacon in a 6 x 4ft room to the rear of the shop, with the sides of bacon hung from hooks in the charred roof over burning sawdust heaped across the floor. Some of his loyal staff remained for fifty years, and it was not until he was in his seventies that Rowland himself finally retired; he died in 1971, and Daisy in 1983. The grocery shop was acquired by International Stores a few years before they in turn sold out in 1959 to Woolworth's, adding to Nos 79 and 80 next door which they had opened seven years earlier.

Rowland Hill moved from Weymouth in 1896 with his wife Louisa, son Rowland jnr (aged eight) and daughter Ada (aged six), upon purchasing Mrs Hewett's grocery business at No. 78 High Street, Lymington, which had been founded by James Hewett in 1878. Rowland jnr became apprenticed in the grocery trade at Weymouth and Guildford, but in 1900 his father died of consumption at the age of thirty-six, so Louisa continued to run the business until 1920, when she emigrated to New Zealand to live with her daughter, Ada Reid. That same year, in St Thomas' church, Rowland jnr married Daisy Russell, who was born in Stockbridge before her

Cecil Barrow was employed as chauffeur to the Earl of Egmont at Avon Castle, but yearned to run his own motorcycle business. After he was married at Ringwood in 1919, his father Harry consented to purchase Mr H.T. Bath's corn and seed merchant's shops at Nos 79-80 High Street, Lymington, for conversion into a motorcycle and cycle sales and repair business. Cecil is pictured on the left in 1925 with mechanics Alf Collins, Midge Haines and Jack Shepherd. As Official ACU Repairer, Cecil installed a BP petrol pump by the front door – with the storage tank under the shop floor – and added wireless sales and repairs.

As a Royal Enfield motorcycle agent, Cecil competed in every Isle of Man TT race between 1925 and '35, his best performance coming in 1928 when averaging 58.92mph in the junior class on an Enfield. He practised at speed on his tuned bikes across Beaulieu Heath, with daughters Betty and Jean coerced as timekeepers. Besides racing at Brooklands and Crystal Palace, Cecil also captained Southampton speedway team from 1928-30. A Lymington Motorcycle Club founder-member, he served as the fastest wartime Home Guard despatch rider for miles around. He formed a syndicate with R. Mason and H. Jones which manufactured around a hundred JMB chain-drive three-wheeled cars, powered by 497cc JAP engines in ash wood frames, which sold for £75 10s, until their generous road tax advantage ended with the 1936 Budget. In 1951 Cecil sold his premises to Woolworth's, whose former staff held a reunion on 13 November 2002, marking fifty years since the store's doors first opened.

The top of Town Hill in 1910. On the immediate right is No. 115 High Street, which was occupied by pork butcher George Bennett and his family for over sixty years. Various traders occupied No. 114 next door before the turn of the century, including confectioner Charles Gooden, A.E. Green the watchmaker, G. Pardey, brick and lime merchant, and Miss King at the time of this photograph.

Seen protruding from the first floor window is the sign Public Telephone Call Office. The mysteries of telegraphy had reached Lymington in 1852, when the service was extended from Brockenhurst station to Lymington. At first the project was not a financial success, for when the Council was asked to meet its debts to the telegraph company, they had to borrow £150 for this and other deficiencies from town clerk James Brown, while town banker Mr St Barbe also loaned money.

Further along is the Red Lion pub, dating from around the 1600s. Next comes the ironmonger's business established by George Hapgood in 1848, which remained in that family until 1981, when it became a card shop, currently a hairdressers. Further along, in Nos 110 and 111, was occupied by George Bennett & Sons drapers and clothier's shops from the mid-1800s; fascinated children would watch as customers' money was placed inside a metal cylinder, which the counter assistant would send by spring-loaded trigger along an overhead cable to the cash desk, whence the cylinder returned with receipt and change. Bennett's operated for almost a century until giving way in 1996 to Tesco, who also took over Willis' grocers shop on the opposite side of the street.

In 1893 the solicitor Herbert Cullin Heppenstall moved south from Nottinghamshire to purchase the practice of Coxwell & Pope at 1 High Street, and set up his own business on the first floor of No. 35 High Street, above George Gidden the saddler and harness maker. Three years later Mr Heppenstall moved to No. 75 (pictured on the immediate right in 1906) where, with a staff of two, he occupied the ground floor rooms, the upstairs being used as a home for his mother and sister. Such was his success that by 1901, with Herbert Clark as partner, branches were opened at Brockenhurst and Milford. In 1915 he also took over the solicitor's business of Henry St Barbe at No. 72 High Street. Within five years a Lyndhurst office was added by Basil Rustom, hence the name Heppenstall Clark & Rustom. New Milton and Highcliffe offices were added in 1923. Owing to clients' increasing mobility through car ownership after the Second World War, Heppenstall's now comprises three offices, at Lymington, New Milton and Lyndhurst, with over forty staff.

Long service amongst Heppenstall's staff has become a byword: Basil Rustom (fifty years), his son Peter Rustom, Jim Burgess, Doris Stanley and Liz Coster (all over forty years) all fall well short of Fred Rogers, clerk for sixty-four years until retiring at the age of eighty. He died aged ninety-five in 1997, three days after being knocked over by a car whilst crossing the High Street. In retirement, Fred invariably saluted every time he passed Heppenstall's office. The staff returned to No. 75 in 2002 after extensive building repairs.

By the mid-1800s Nos 53 and 54 High Street, The Red House and Home Mead, formed a house, premises and pleasure ground. Sisters Miss Harriet Spike and Mrs Fanny Haldane inherited Home Mead from their father Edward Spike, and in 1908 Harriet bequeathed £4,000 and the residue of her estate 'for the purchase of a site, and the building, or aiding to build, of an additional church in Lymington, on condition that an equal amount be raised by subscription or otherwise.' Fanny left her estate for the same purpose, so that their combined £18,000 represented the greatest bequest for ecclesiastical purposes in the town. This enabled the construction of All Saints' church and hall at Woodside. The first curate there, in 1910, was the Revd E. Utterton. In February 2000, Lymington Methodists, having vacated their own church founded in Gosport Street in 1859, signed a declaration of partnership to share All Saints' for Sunday services, which was refurbished in 2002 from the proceeds of the Methodists' sale.

Home Mead (as pictured) enjoyed uninterrupted rear views across the Solent. During the First World War it was requisitioned as an eighty-five bed hospital for wounded New Zealand troops sent back from the front lines in France, nursed by Lymington St John's members. Later, Home Mead accommodated the private Mersley School until requisitioned as a furniture store in the Second World War. In 1960, by compulsory purchase, the property was demolished and replaced by the town's main post office. Lymington's first post office was situated at 88 High Street, followed by Nos 84, 72 and, from 1905, No. 55 High Street, currently a Job Centre.

A fine view of a dirt-tracked St Thomas'
Street. The dress shop which now stands on
the site of the first two cottages on the left is
probably one of the oldest in this part of
Lymington, dating from around 1620. The
properties next door now form a chemist's shop.
This was, on either side of the Second World
War, Doe's the confectioners and a café, run by
the wife of 'Mosey' Doe, the town chimney
sweep (inset). Invariably covered in soot, Mosey
built himself a primitive motorised contraption
in which to carry his sweep's brushes and sacks of
soot, with tiller steering and bodywork hinged at
the front, which was lifted to gain entry. This
noisy three-wheeler was kept in a rickety garage
at the bottom of his field midway along the
northern side of Middle Road. When the vehicle
was removed upon Mosey's death, the
unfortunate occupants' feet fell straight through
its floorboards.

On the opposite side of the street stands the
imposing private residences of Quadrille Court,
named after the favourite card game played by
French officers who were billeted there. From the

Chapter 2

ST THOMAS'
STREET

start of the French Revolution to the end of the
Napoleonic Wars, many French emigrants
landed in Lymington, with several regiments
stationed around the town. The quarters of the
600 men in the Royal (French) Marine
commanded by Count d'Hector were stationed at
Buckland, while Col. Rochalier's French artillery
occupied the Malthouse and nearby buildings in
New Lane (now New Street). Many of the
French stayed on long after the Revolution
ended.

Thankfully most of the old façades remain in St Thomas' Street. One notable exception is No. 4, seen pictured in 1878 when this was the imposing shop front of W. Torah, dealer in works of art, clocks and chinaware. Statuettes and flowering plants feature prominently in his display. Following the demolition of this shop, the plot lay as an open-grassed area, with a wooden shed to the rear, which remained a favoured spot for open-air dances, until the Lyric cinema was opened there in 1913. Nowadays it is the Waitrose supermarket site.

No. 1 St Thomas' Street, pictured, is Monmouth House, a property of considerable architectural significance, built around 1650 with two-inch brickwork, thick window bars and stone doorway. During the Monmouth Rebellion of 1685 this site was the home of Mrs Knapton, a lady of considerable ingenuity. There was a strong party of Monmouth's supporters at Lymington at that time, accustomed to meeting in Mrs Knapton's house. On one occasion a party of the King's men forced an entry during such a meeting, but the conspirators affected their escape through the rear windows. Showing commendable presence of mind, Mrs Knapton wrapped a piece of flannel around her head and puffed furiously on one of the discarded clay pipes, persuading the soldiers this was the only cure for her persistent toothache. Monmouth House is now a rest home, with the local owners Colten spending a considerable sum maintaining the property in its original style.

In 1840 Charles Ford (inset) and his wife Emma arrived from Southampton to open their furniture shop at Nos 47-48 St Thomas' Street, next to Lymington parish church. In their 'extensive showrooms' they offered 'Bedsteads and bedding, carpets and rugs, floor-cloths, linoleums, mats, drawing room, sitting room and bedroom suites, general furnishing, marine store dealers.' They lived over the shop, and with their son Charles jnr taking no interest, their daughter Sarah joined the business. She went on to marry Alfred Isted, who later became a partner in the shop, and furniture removals were added to their venture.

After Charles snr died in 1902, and Alfred the following year, Sarah took over the firm, together with her three children Charles, Alfred and Vera. In 1905 they acquired 61 and 62 High Street on the opposite side of the road. Sarah and Vera were left in control when the menfolk were called up for First World War service. Eight members of the two Isted families were conscripted for Second World War duties, two of whom were killed, and in 1941 the St Thomas' Street shop was destroyed by an incendiary bomb. It was rebuilt in 1961.

Alan and Geoff Isted, together with their cousins Ken and Patricia Isted and Geoff's son Roger, continued to operate the Ford's enterprise until Geoff, the last active survivor, retired and sold up to Geoff Kemp and Terry Palfrey in 1997.

Subsequent films, and performances by Lymington Philharmonic Society, were accompanied by a piano costing £30. Sunday evening films began in 1919, defying strong condemnation by the vicar. The cinema overcame temporary opposition in 1921 from the People's Theatre at the Literary Institute in New Street, but the popularity of television led to the Lyric's eventual closure in June 1963.

Meantime two local men employed by the agricultural merchants SCATS, lorry driver Ken Porter who became the Lymington Shop manager, and Tom Clark, a labourer before managing machinery sales at Sway, decided to set up their own corn and seed merchants' business in Queen Street in 1953. Porter & Clark then moved to No. 17 St Thomas' Street, before acquiring the empty Lyric cinema for £19,000 in 1965, with conversion into a large store, retaining the cinema's sloping floor. The premises became a Waitrose supermarket in 1970, which was extended in 2000 by acquiring the adjoining Marks' bakery shop, earlier owned by the House family.

The grassed area of No. 4 St Thomas' Street was a favoured site for open-air dances until, in 1913, Lymington & New Forest Entertainments Ltd accepted the High Street builders Rashley's tender of £1,768 10s to construct the Lyric cinema there. This opened in December with Mr Dibley as film operator and Miss Pelfrey cashier, with ten rows of seating at 3d, six at 6d, three at 1s, and three at 1s 6d. The following February the cinema was closed for roof strengthening, and the manager Mr Elgar was fired for lack of smartness and unseemly conduct towards young female patrons.

For fifteen years Fredrick William House managed the High Street furnisher's workshop of Mr E.R. Badcock, owner of numerous commercial concerns in the town, including the mercer and draper's shop at Nos 41-42 High Street, as well as the estate agency, furniture and undertaker's at Nos 91-92. Mourners requesting Badcock's personal presence at a funeral, wearing a silk hat and walking in front of the horse-drawn hearse, were charged an extra £10. In 1897 Frederick House (pictured) took the bold decision to set up business on his own, ignoring Mr Badcock's taunts that he would be asking for his job back within six months. Initially he agreed to rent No. 33 St Thomas' Street from a retired farmer John Tiler Moore at a rent of £18, and early in 1898 he advertised in *The Popular Advertiser* that he had commenced business as an upholsterer and undertaker, in addition to making blinds, beating and relaying carpets, cleaning, re-carding and remaking mattresses, and doing pinking in all sizes. No. 34 St Thomas' Street was at first rented, before both Nos 33-34 were purchased in 1938 from the

executors of the late Revd Harry New for £1,300, thus creating a double-fronted shop.

The garage premises next door were occupied by The South Coast Paint Co. with the Misses Banks' private school for young ladies in the rooms above; both Nos 35 and 36 were purchased in 1933 by Charles House for £1,120 from architect John Bevis.

The business continues today in the fourth generation. Whereas original clients made their final journey by horse-drawn hearse, they are conveyed now in a new Rolls Royce Silver Spirit.

In 1911 the Hobby family patriotically festooned their bakery at No. 25 St Thomas' Street, at the junction with Belmore Lane, to mark the Coronation of King George V. From left to right: Arthur Harry Hobby; his brother Walter, a Royal Navy master-at-arms who served in the China Seas; his wife Fanny; Herbert Hobby. The family bakery business was founded in 1870 by Harry Hobby in nearby Stanford Road, before occupying this shop, leased from Mrs St Barbe of Romsey. The two bread-baking ovens were fuelled by locally-collected bundles of hazel-rod faggots. Bread was delivered around Lymington and Pennington, and when Mr Hobby acquired a high-roofed cart drawn by a cab, he was taunted by local boys who remarked upon its similarity to a hearse.

Arthur (born 1865) married twenty-year-old Anne Adams of Barton in 1890, and took over the running of the business on his father's death in 1908, while Herbert was also involved before emigrating to New Zealand. Arthur died in 1948, and Anne ran the business until her death in 1963, at the age of ninety-three. The shop was then rented to a taxi firm for a few years, before the site was sold to Hampshire Motorways. As a sitting tenant Arthur's son, Edwin, ran his shoe-mending business from a small dwelling at the bottom of the garden until he died in 1966. Hampshire Motorways sold out to Excelsior Coaches of Bournemouth, who used the site as a pick-up point and ticket office – for years remaining an eyesore with huge rusting RSJ girders. Protracted planning wrangles ended in 1998 with permission to erect thirteen three-storey flats above shops on the site.

The Westwood family came from Southampton when Frank Westwood opened his hardware shop at No. 26 St Thomas' Street (extreme left); he also owned several cottages around the corner in Queen Street. He advertised his oils, paints, tin, iron, galvanised and enamelled ware, and walked to the bank with the daily takings wrapped in old newspaper. Frank was succeeded by his son Clement 'Windy' Dyer, who delivered paraffin on his bike as far as East Boldre, besides pedalling on Continental holidays with friend Walt Lee. The Westwoods converted the cottage next door into a grocery shop, and beyond that at No. 26a is Mr Knight's high-class confectionery shop, later acquired by Bert Cox. Walter Arnold arrived from Basingstoke to open his South Hants Coach Works at No. 27 in 1896, announcing that 'Any type of Motor Body built to order. Repairs completed with care and dispatch at reasonable prices.' He later sold out to Fred Keeping, the established garage proprietor at Milford.

The next row of cottages were demolished for the Co-operative Wholesale Society's grocery and butcher's stores, built much further back from the pavement as the Council planned to widen the street, which came to nought. The shop premises at No. 28, seen behind the handcart, was owned by three generations of Benjamin Winseys. The first was a painter and decorator until his death at the age of fifty-one, his son then converted the front room into a shoemaker's workroom and shop, before being succeeded in turn by the third generation Benjamin, assisted by his wife Freda hand-sewing the shoe uppers, before they retired in 1977 and sold the shop, now Papworths jewellers. On the right is pictured Thomas Habgood's boot and shoe factory.

Moore, Trestrail & Blatch at No. 38 High Street.

Without warning, Dr Kay declared his intention to retire with immediate effect. This left Dr Pitt in quite a predicament, until 'Purple' and his partners agreed they should bid for Bellevue House and its magnificent garden, as it came up for public auction in 1951 at the Angel Hotel, upon direction of the marriage settlement trustees of Dr Kay and his wife, who had died after falling from an upstairs window onto the patio. The solicitors successfully acquired the property for £7,500, and sold off the adjoining former coach-house to Drs Pitt and Sam Johnson for their surgery. In 1982 this cramped practice, with 8,000 patients, moved to the three-storey Chawton House in St Thomas' Street, which dates back to 1730. But by 2002 this building too was inadequate, so Dr Tom McEwen and his partners added the pub next door, joined by a two-storey linkway. Opened in 1836 as The Fighting Cocks, the pub had been closed by magistrate Col Hammersley in 1882 for unruly behaviour, only allowed to reopen when the name was changed to The Dorset Arms.

In 1902 Dr Charles Kay opened his practice at the imposing Georgian residence Bellevue House, No. 48, High Street (seen centre-right of this photograph taken from the church tower). He once holidayed in Vienna, returning with an opera singer on his arm. Dr Kay took on Dr George Pitt as the practice's surgeon, who had just returned from serving in the French trenches during the First World War. He lived in a flat at the nearby Old Bank House, where another occupier was Cecil 'Purple' Blatch, a partner in the solicitors

Fred Butcher arrived at Lymington in 1920 as manager of W.R. Fletcher, the butcher's shop at No. 125 High Street, thereby following a family tradition. Fred's grandfather had served as a butcher in the Army, and his father ran a butcher's shop in Southampton where as a young lad Fred, one of twelve children, was made to stand in the shop window on Saturday afternoons shouting out bargains to passers-by, for without fridges the meat would be unsaleable by Monday. Fred joined Fletcher the Southampton butcher before promotion to manager of their Lymington town hill branch, No.125 High Street, where his first week's takings amounted to £37, when breast of lamb was sold for 3d per pound. The assistant manager was Frank Bennett, who had given up his own little butcher's shop in Sway.

With seven other traditional butchers in the town centre, Fred and Frank started their own business in 1948 after purchasing Nos 13-14 St Thomas' Street from Sid Prichard, a short man who wore a straw boater, his butcher's shop floor covered in sawdust to soak up blood dripping from carcasses. Butcher & Bennett continued until the partners both retired in 1969, when Fred's son Doug took over the business, later joined by his own son Mike, by now Butcher & Butcher the butchers. In 1988 Mike, as the fifth generation, took charge of the business, but although showing an annual rise in profits despite competition from three major supermarkets, he felt forced to close the shop in February 2003.

Monmouth House, in St Thomas' Street, commands considerable architectural significance, built around 1650 with a 2ft brickwork and stone doorway. Mrs Knapton lived there during the 1685 Rebellion, and one night the Monmouth supporters met here, escaping through the rear windows as the King's men forced entry. The house later became the Vicarage and the Revd Ellis Jones lived there. This was followed by a further change of use, as the home and practice surgery of Dr Maturin,

together with his partners Gilbert Stewart, de Mowbray (whose four sons all became doctors), and Basil Thornton. The latter purchased 'Wistaria' on the opposite side of the street as his family home (pictured): a 1740 building with a false Georgian frontage hung with mathematical tiles covered with Wistaria.

When Dr Maturin retired not long after the Second World War, the practice of Drs Thornton, Stewart and Hamish Allen moved into Wistaria. The group also included Dr John Salkield in Milford and Dr Ken Martin at Brockenhurst, who carried out his routine visits in a Rolls-Royce bequeathed by a patient. Over the years this grew into a joint practice of 13,500 patients, 8,500 in Lymington and the remainder at Milford. By now bulging at the seams, a new £1½ million Wistaria health centre was opened in November 2002 (next to the graveyard!) under senior partner Anthea McAlister, complete with pharmacy, Social Services presence, and a private lease for a new local Red Cross headquarters.

The Manor of Pennington is one of the most ancient in Hampshire, for a long time held in undivided thirds by three different owners, an arrangement which continued until comparatively modern times. In 1803 the estate passed into the hands of the Tomline family, from whom it was acquired in 1834 by John Pulteney. He and his wife Elizabeth were great benefactors to Pennington, especially its church and school, whilst their son Keppel Pulteney provided a soup kitchen building in Wainsford Road to mark Queen Victoria's Diamond Jubilee in 1897, with soup dispensed for 1d per quart, as well as land for Lymington's new hospital which opened in 1913 as a memorial to King Edward VII.

The name Pennington is derived from 'a farm which paid a penny rate.' In 1932 the Vicar, the Revd L.A. Hughes, purchased farmland off Lodge Road for the purpose of a village recreation ground; he also bought the turf sods which were

Chapter 3

PENNINGTON

laid by the newly-formed Pennington Cricket Club. The village retained its individuality, shown by this 1922 aerial photograph, and was served by its own Parish Council, until swallowed up into the Lymington Borough in 1932. The construction of vast council house estates after the war, the first in Corbin Road and Pennington Oval, ultimately led to Pennington physically merging with Lymington.

Pennington village centre, 1904, in days when parishioners were proud of their independence and not obligated to Lymington in any way. Pictured on the left is a domestic servant collecting water at the hand-primed parish pump, whilst buildings on the right end at the Sportsman's Arms. The shop on the left was occupied by Mr G. Rogers, baker, grocer and corn merchant, whose bread was delivered daily in a horse-drawn van, whilst on Friday afternoons, before his ovens had cooled, he baked cakes made by customers themselves. Much village gossip was exchanged at Pennington post office and village store, on the corner with Wainsford Road, while social functions were hosted in the large Victoria Room above that shop. One Pennington family of long standing, descendants of the French Huguenots, were the Tizards, dating back to Joseph Tizard's arrival in 1841. He married Charlotte Saunders in the old Pennington church; they lived in Wainsford Road and had seven offspring. Employed by the Government as a skilled carver in wood and stone, Joseph was employed as Clerk of Works when Hurst Castle lighthouse was rebuilt in 1850. One son, Herbert Edward, was appointed organist and choirmaster at St Mark's from 1890 to 1903. His daughter Joan married a local horticulturist Alfred Stephens at St Mark's in 1940; she continued to live in Pennington until becoming resident at a Lymington rest home in 2002.

That same year New Forest District Council provoked much friction within Pennington when installing traffic-calming measures, with 'build-outs' to the immediate north and south of The Square (pictured) designed to reduce traffic speed – many villagers contending this simply increased dangers and congestion.

Educational facilities in Pennington were somewhat primitive, with children taught in four private houses before this school was opened in Pennington Square in September 1852, thanks to a benefactor, Mrs Evelyn Pulteney, lady of the manor. She donated the site plus £1,300 towards construction, the remaining £300 being collected by the Revd William Lambert, inducted Vicar of Pennington in 1848. A clock was erected in the bell-tower by Pennington folk to mark the Coronation of King George V. The first headmaster was James Lockett, with his wife the first mistress in a joint appointment. The building was soon outgrown, so an infant school was built nearby in 1886-87. Generations of Pennington children were taught at these schools until, in 1960, two classrooms of the new school in Priestlands Road were occupied, and by Christmas 1970 the remaining staff and children also occupied the completed eight-classroom school.

On 10 September 2002, Pennington Junior school staff and pupils wore Victorian costume to mark the school's 150th anniversary, led by the head teacher Hilary Flaxman. The children chanted multiplication tables, played in segregated playgrounds for boys and girls, heard reminiscences from former Pennington teachers and pupils, and the Bishop of Winchester, Michael Scott-Joynt, gave an animated address in St Mark's church. In addition they were shown around the old school by the present owner, antiques auctioneer George Kidner.

Pennington Common has been the scene for much village entertainment over the years, and a more sinister happening. The village football and cricket clubs competed on the Lower Common, before the vicar, the Revd L.A. Hughes, generously defrayed the purchase of farmland to create Pennington recreation ground in 1932. Children played on the Common alongside vast numbers of grazing donkeys, hence the soubriquet 'Donkey Town'. A large pond bordering Ramley Road often froze over during the winter, attracting skaters from a wide area.

Village women dried and aired their laundry on the gorse bushes, with some taking in washing to supplement the family's meagre income. Such was the remarkable variety of wild flowers to be seen on the forty-five acre Common around 1920 that Pennington School headmaster Thomas Pattenden meticulously counted no fewer than 123 different species. It is now an SSSI managed by the Town Council, who introduced play equipment.

On Wednesday 13 April 1814, Pennington Common was the scene of the Army's last duel. Capt. William Souper felt insulted by Lt John Dietrich and, receiving no apology, challenged him to a pistol duel by Lymington River. When a constable appeared, the combatants rode by post-chaise to the Common, where Dietrich was first to fire but missed his adversary, before himself suffering a wound from the right hip to the backbone. Despite surgery in Lymington Hospital, he died within two days. Souper was found guilty of murder at Hampshire Assizes, where Mr Justice Dampier pronounced death by hanging, with a recommendation for clemency. Souper soon returned to his Army career, from which he retired in 1835.

The ladies of Pennington Women's Institute held their inaugural meeting on January 23 1923, at the village school in Pennington Square, where they remained whilst their own hall was under construction further along Ramley Road, at the junction with Yaldhurst Lane and Lodge Road. The original plans drawn up by architect Mr J. Bevir showed a thatched roof, but when sheaves were laid along the roof ready to be pinned down, a storm blew up scattering the straw reeds, so the ladies decided to opt for a tiled roof. The 250-seater hall was duly completed by local builder F. Pearce at a cost of around £1,800. There was much rejoicing when the hall was formally opened on October 14 1925, by founder-president Miss Helen Fullerton. A plaque declares it to have been built by fellow members, relations and friends in loving memory of the WI's first treasurer and original member Lady Nora Brand.

During the Second World War the hall car park was cultivated so that members could grow potatoes for the national Dig for Victory campaign. The P-WITS drama group was formed in the 1960s with Dorothy Waters as producer, and continues to entertain locals with up to twenty pantomimes and shows for Forest care homes and local organisations each winter. The Institute also entered Lymington carnival. Principal guest at their diamond jubilee in 1983 was WI national chairman Mrs Ann Harris. That same year a new £2,367 heating system was installed, the coke fire giving way to radiators. Four years later a new roof was erected for £15,000. Membership now stands at sixty-five.

THE BAND STAND
LYMINGTON 21.

For years, crowds of Lymington families loved to while away their summer Sunday afternoons on the Bath Road riverfront park, with young children sailing their toy yachts on the two boating pools – one being the stormwater balancing pond near the Sea Water Baths, long since covered in concrete as a dinghy park. In those sedate days crowds would listen to Lymington Military Band perform regular concerts in the Victorian bandstand. Alas, this structure mysteriously disappeared during the Second World War, raising various theories regarding its loss. It was not until the year 2000 that a substantial new £65,000 bandstand reappeared on the same site, as Lymington Town Council's recognition of the Millennium – no doubt influenced by town clerk Ray Jones, deputy bandmaster with Boscombe Salvation Army Band.

Seen sailing along the river into Lymington is the tug *Carrier* which, along with the *Jumsey*, hauled specially constructed tow-boats which looked like half-barges with a gate across one end. They were introduced in May 1836, so that ferry passengers did not have to share the decks with frightened animals. The year 1913 saw 700 cars land at Yarmouth in this manner, as the Lymington route was far more popular and convenient for motorists than the Portsmouth-Ryde crossing. By 1930 the number had risen to 1,650 vehicles, the tow-boats finally succumbing to double-ended car ferries in 1938.

Inevitably there have been collisions in and
outside the Lymington River. The most serious
incident came on 25 April 1908, when a blizzard
left the town's streets under several feet of snow.
Out in the Solent, between Yarmouth and
Lymington, such conditions led to a maritime
disaster. The Royal Navy's 5,750-ton cruiser
HMS *Gladiator* had left Portland with 250 men,
bound for Portsmouth, while the 11,630-ton
American express mail liner *St Paul* had steamed
out of Southampton in the opposite direction for
New York. The two ships were less than half a
mile apart when, through the snowstorm, their
look-outs realised they were on a collision
course, the *St Paul* proceeding at thirteen knots,
the Gladiator at nine. Capt. Passow correctly
swung the *St Paul* hard to port, after stopping his
engines. Lieut. Mainguy also ordered the
Gladiator to port – but when both ships' sirens
blasted simultaneously, the cruiser's officers
thought the *St Paul* had sounded twice, signifying
she was going to port. As the liner's bows headed
for the *Gladiator* amidships, too late Capt.
Lumsden shouted 'Hard a port'.

Men in the Navy mess room were killed, many
injured, stokers buried under coal, and others

Chapter 4

THE RIVER AND SOLENT

thrown across the ship. When the *St Paul* went
into reverse, the flooded Gladiator keeled over to
starboard. Around fifty sailors attempted to swim
250 yards to be met by Royal Engineers wading
out from Fort Victoria, while the remaining crew
climbed on to the upturned hull before
evacuating on to the *St Paul*. The next day Capt.
Lumsden reported one Lieutenant and twenty-
eight men dead. It took five months and £50,000
to strip the *Gladiator* of her armaments and raise
the hull, before she was sold to a breaker for
£15,125. Ten years to the very day after the
collision, the *St Paul* suddenly capsized and sank
whilst at anchor in New York.

LYMINGTON
TOWN & HARBOUR

Sailing craft gave way to steam between Lymington and Yarmouth with the arrival of the 58ft wooden paddle steamer *Glasgow*, which entered regular service on 5 April 1830, passengers sharing the decks with cargo and animals. Several local businessmen carried on this enterprise until the Solent Sea Steam Packet Co. was formed in 1842, a year after the arrival of the Southampton-built 82ft wooden *Solent*. By 1884 R. Dore commanded the *Glasgow* and J. Cribb the *Solent*. In 1858 the 76ft *Red Lion* joined the fleet, then in 1863 a new 94ft *Solent* (pictured left) replaced her namesake, followed by the 98ft *Mayflower* (right) in 1866. By now, as the Solent Steampacket Co., tow-boats had been added to carry carriages, horses, cattle and heavy goods at 'very moderate prices.' Fares were Lymington-Yarmouth 1s 6d on the quarter-deck, 1s forecastle, or corresponding day tickets 2s and 1s 6d. Airing tickets (non-landing) were 1s. During the 1850s Alfred Lord Tennyson, who lived at Farringford on the Isle of Wight, wrote his inspirational poem Crossing the Bar on the Lymington-Yarmouth passage, while in 1896 Guglielmo Marconi hired the *Solent* and *Mayflower* to carry out his ship-to-shore telegraphy experiments with the Needles Hotel.

Pictured in the foreground is the wooden pontoon constructed at the turn of the century by Lymington Shipyard shipwright George Turrell. Here Mr E.R. Badcock's rowing boats landed for the halfpenny crossing from the Quay, or for a penny further along to Ferry Point House.

Lymington has a long history in shipbuilding, instanced by the medieval ship incorporated in the town's seal. The present boatyard site was occupied by boat-builder John Rogerys in 1513, and 154 years later Charles Guidot sold this 2½-acre yard to John Coombes. Trading vessels up to sixty tons, and Government revenue cutters, were principal orders. An experimental submarine was built there in 1804, probably the first in England, designed by an American inventor Robert Fulton. In 1819 the boatbuilder Thomas Inman arrived from Hastings to take over the boatyard, and went on to build several trophy-winning vessels for the Weld family, including the *Alarm* in 1830, later lengthened into an 248-ton schooner, one of the few to beat the celebrated *America* which took the Queen's Cup back to the States and renamed it the America's Cup. This detailed painting depicts the construction of the 377-ton *Fortuna* in the new boatshed, launched in 1877, the largest vessel ever to be built on the Lymington River.

The boatyard changed hands several times before being acquired by Mr H.G. May in 1918,

who brought his Berthon Boat Co. there. Military vessels built during the Second World War included minesweepers and MTBs. The business is now run by his great-grandsons Brian and Dominic May, employing 130 including staff on the 250-berth marina. Fitting out RNLI lifeboats, twenty-one in the fifteen years up until 2002 when contracts were signed for two more at £2 million apiece, is a major contributor towards the £10-million annual turnover.

Lymington Pier and Harbour, with one solitary moored yacht, 1909. Beyond is the track, opened on 1 May 1884 by the London & South Western Railway, extending the line from Lymington Town station to Lymington Pier and enabling the cross-Solent ferries to operate at all states of the tide. Seen at the Pier is the paddle-steamer Solent, which had been introduced in March 1902, the third vessel of this name to operate on the Lymington-Yarmouth service, yet offering far greater comfort for passengers with its extensive-covered accommodation. The Pier had its own railway signal box, along with the distinction of the longest single-span railway crossing gate in the country. The year 1923 saw the formation of the Southern Railway Company, with their 'push and pull' steam engines to Brockenhurst. Steam trains gave way to the electrified line in 1967.

Today presents a very different picture. As a very busy yachting centre, Lymington Harbour Commissioners, a non-profit-making body comprising river users and local councillors, administer activities on the river through a Harbourmaster and chief executive. There is a speed limit of six knots along the river and anchoring is prohibited; visitors sail straight for Town Quay with its 140 berths. In addition there are 1,500 permanent moorings, with 600 at Lymington Yacht Haven marina, 250 at the Berthon marina, and 650 managed by the Harbour Commissioners, including 79 on their Fortuna Dock.

Lymington's commodious sea-water baths, using an inlet from the salterns, date back to at least 1755, when bathing-house proprietor Mr Milford was summoned for not paying a 4d rate. During his tours around the country, acclaimed fine draughtsman and humorist Thomas Rowlandson stayed at the Angel Hotel in 1784, and his Lymington sketches included 'Mrs Beeston's strengthening Baths'. Advertised charges in 1825 were: a warm bath 3s 6d, shower 2s 6d, a cold bath with a guide 1s, without a guide 6d (male guides kept swimmers afloat by holding them up with a rope). The public Lymington Bath & Improvement Company was formed in 1833, extending the baths by enclosing a large tract of mud land, raising £6,000 through £25 shares and donations. The present building, with separate wings for ladies and gentlemen, and upper circular room for social gatherings, was designed by local architect William Bartlett. After the Company got into difficulties in around 1855, the Baths were sold cheaply to shipbuilder George Inman, before personal extravagances led to the whole of his estate being sold.

Thanks to the generosity of the Lymington industrialist John Howlett, the Baths were acquired by the local Corporation in 1929. The 1933 photograph shows swimming instructor Mr Simpson on the left, his assistant wife on the right, with civic dignitaries and firemen. Now operated by the Town Council's fourteen part-time staff from May to September, the 300 x 100ft pool holds 1.37 million gallons of filtered seawater.

The lower deck was then scrubbed to remove all coal dust. At the end of each crossing the *Freshwater* would be swung before tying up, ready to travel in the opposite direction. On request from their owners, the fireman would cremate dead pets in the ship's boiler; he always shovelled overboard the previous day's ashes. The *Freshwater* is pictured taking part at the Naval Review in the Solent on 16 July 1935. Her service at Lymington ended in 1959.

With the volume of barge-towed motor vehicles causing operational problems, the revolutionary Clyde-built double-ended car ferry *Lymington* entered service in 1938, the first British ferry with Voith-Schneider propulsion, making rudders superfluous. Further evolution has led to today's 190ft sister-ships, the *Caedmon* (launched 1973), *Cenwulf* (1973) and *Cenred* (1974), each costing £1.8 million and able to carry 750 passengers and 52 cars. With Sealink giving way to Wightlink, in 2001 they carried 1,335,155 foot passengers, 345,433 cars, 2,987 coaches and 31,991 commercial freight vehicles on the Lymington-Yarmouth passage. The *Cenred* is seen dressed on 7 June 1980 to mark the ferry crossing's 150th anniversary.

Increasing demand in ferry traffic to Yarmouth led to the elegant paddle steamer *Freshwater* arriving as Lymington's largest vessel in 1927, after her launch from the boatyard of J. Samuel White in Cowes. She had a promenade deck extending three-quarters of her 159ft length and enclosed shelter below, including first-class lounge aft, saloon bar and ladies' room forward; her contract speed was 11½ knots. Bunkering was performed in the early hours of the morning, with fifteen tons of coal taken aboard, brought alongside on barges towed by a Southern Railway motor-boat and passed across in wicker baskets.

Lymington was a busy port when, in 1345 at the request of Edward III, the town provided nine ships and 159 men for his defences, almost double that of Portsmouth. Such seamen frequented the many ale houses around the Quay. And with Lymington a principal manufacturer of salt for 700 years, ships of up to 1,300 tons took advantage of the double tides in the deep river to berth at the Quay, offloading coal needed to burn off the salt – indeed around 1660, Lymington unloaded as much coal for the salterns as was handled in London. Timber was imported from Scandinavia, along with fish and fur from Newfoundland. Coal yards remained along this stretch of the Quay beyond the First World War, when a dozen or more men would run up one gangplank and down another, carrying coal in basket-skips – some of which 'inadvertently' fell into the River, to be retrieved furtively after nightfall.

The Solent was noted for piracy until the eighteenth century when smuggling became a more profitable venture. Brandy kegs and silks would be buried in mud along the Pennington coastline whenever the alarm was raised, or sunk on a line over the side of the ship, before being brought ashore hidden in carts with false flatbeds. When Daniel Defoe visited Lymington in 1727 he complained bitterly that 'rogueing and smuggling' was a major industry, declaring: 'I do not find that they have any foreign commerce except it be what we call smuggling.' Several of the town's forty-five inns acted as surreptitious headquarters.

The introduction of the 120ft steamer *Lymington* on 6 April 1893 marked the first addition to the Lymington-Yarmouth fleet for twenty-seven years. Launched at Southampton from the boatyard of Day, Summers & Co., she entered service at the 3 p.m. sailing from Lymington Pier on 9 May, with Capt. Seymour (pictured third from right) transferring from the *Mayflower* in order to take command, and Mr G. Cottrell as engineer. The *Lymington*, with its open wheelhouse and shining brasses on the cowling, could accommodate 311 passengers within the limits of the Solent, or 274 for excursions as far as Newhaven and Weymouth. It was on one such excursion, on 13 August 1909, that this photograph was taken. On the extreme left is ferry steward Harry Doe jnr, who had earlier served on the *Mayflower*. Against advice, Harry later sailed his yacht across the Solent in rough weather in order to carry a doctor to Yarmouth; returning with his mate Jack Clark on board, both were drowned in the storm, their bodies washed up off Lepe. Standing alongside Harry is Mrs Annie Sparkes, who ran Broad Lane Stores for customers in this southern part of Lymington, the shop proving particularly popular with children for the range of sweets it had to offer.

In November 2002, Andy Lavies retired after skippering Lymington-Yarmouth ferries for thirty-three consecutive years, with the dubious distinction of demolishing Yarmouth Pier whilst attempting to berth in 1970 during a force nine gale. A merchant seaman for forty-six years after running away to sea as a fifteen-year-old, he is pictured fourth from the right on his final retirement passage, along with Wightlink's other Lymington masters, including their first female master on this run, Wendy Maugham.

Lymington River rescue of a different sort; a horse and cart slithered over the mudbank, before being brought safely back to dry land. Seen in the background is the old wooden Coastguard boathouse, on the site owned by Lymington Council. Early in 1914, keen sailor Capt. H.H. Nicholson, of Creek Cottage, formed the Lymington River Sailing Club, with eighteen members racing Lymington Pram dinghies built by Dan Bran in his riverside shed for £20, but the outbreak of the First World War that August spelt the Club's closure. In 1921, Major Cyril Potter invited six men and four ladies to a meeting at his house, Blake's (now Ferry Point), and the proposal to re-form the LRSC was unanimously approved, with subs of one guinea a year. Racing resumed on 3 June 1922, and more yachting classes were added. In 1923 the Club was granted the Council's lease to take over the Coastguard boathouse, with the site, shed and slipway costing £600.

By 1928 membership reached 384, and local builder G. Harvey added a second storey to form a large clubroom. In 1926 the LRSC became the Lymington Yacht Club, when application was also made for a Royal Warrant, eventually granted by King George VI in 1938. Lymington XOD yacht division is the third oldest of its class, dating back to 1927. The Club introduced waterborne judges for instant decisions during match-racing, now adopted worldwide. Emphasis has been placed on junior sailing, with 300 youngsters regularly attending Wednesday open training sessions.

the twelve crew to be placed on the telephone for call-outs, but this proved impractical, so it was arranged for Lymington police to fire rockets from iron pipes stuck into the police-station garden. When this was deemed dangerous, compressed-air horns were brought into use. George's first rescue boat was the 26ft twin-engined all-aluminium *Torshent*, which proved a failure, losing her plane with every ripple and only capable of fifteen knots rather than the stipulated thirty. She was superseded successively by the 23ft *Fairey Huntress Maid of Baltimore*, 28ft *McLannahan*, the *Seeker* and finally the *Salty* – all George's own property, with the *Salty* later donated to the junior Salterns Sailing Club. In its first three years the Service cost George almost £35,000, saving over fifty lives, with just one offering a half-crown contribution!

He gave way to Lymington's RNLI inshore station in 1965, with their D-class inflatable (pictured above) stored under a tarpaulin behind the car park hedge until a boathouse was built in 1978. Other Lymington lifeboats named after their donors have been the D-class *Abbey Life*, 21ft *Atlantic Surrey Forester*, and the 21ft *Atlantic Frank and Mary Atkinson*, which answered 388 call-outs before the arrival of the Atlantic 75 *Victor Danny Lovelock*, pictured, being dedicated and named in September 2002.

The first voluntary lifeboat service in the River was set up by the 9th Lymington Sea Scouts in 1937. Twenty-six years later local councillor George McL. Power, who had first owned a Lymington Scow dinghy as a lad, formed his own Sea Rescue Service. He paid for

Conscripted Lymington men served their country across the globe during the Second World War, and upon their return several expressed the wish to form a sailing club, many of them ex-9th Lymington Sea Scouts. Coincidentally, Lymington Borough Council was considering demolishing its sadly dilapidated Bath House property by the river, which had been part of the town's sea water baths dating back to at least the 1780s. Following a public meeting in the High Street town hall, it was agreed Bath House should be rented to a newly-formed Lymington Town Sailing Club. The original forty members faced a mammoth task renovating the derelict octagonal building, where the old plunge baths and boiler house filled at every high tide. Nevertheless the valiant few, led principally by Alan Figgures, spent all their spare hours on this huge task in a spirit of great camaraderie.

Once established, activities afloat led to the formation of an Oxey Bird class, and by 1956 membership reached 480. When a builder Mike Corbin was elected commodore in 1970, urgent measures were taken to remedy the poor condition of the clubhouse, with its leaking roof. Members contributed £24,000 towards a handsome new clubroom with panoramic views across the Solent, to the design of eminent local architect Roger Pinckney. Over the years the Club has made its mark by nurturing many national, international and world racing champions, besides hosting prestigious events.

On the eastern side of the river, opposite Town Quay, were twelve salt pans owned by the brick manufacturer James Burt. Major Jobling built an entertainments theatre there, along with a landing place for theatregoers ferried across from the Quay. As this infringed the rights of the ancient ferry proprietors, the theatre closed within a year or so, and was sold in 1926 for conversion into the Lymington Laundry. Mrs Fitzpatrick was manageress over some fifty staff, with rows of washing hung outside on clothes lines. Thomas Rich, greengrocer on town hill, acted as receiving agent, while covered vans collected and delivered around the New Forest. The premises were acquired in 1936 by Mr Pigott, then in 1958 by Nelson Ewer who, with son Chris, employed up to eighty staff at his Lymington Machine Works, manufacturing presses for such items as Rolls-Royce jet-engine blades and Ford Cortina car rear lights.

In 1984 the site was purchased by Bill Green and Ian King who, following the closure of Jeremy Rogers' Boatyard on the opposite side of the river two years earlier where they played key roles, founded their own Green Marine business in a rented 100ft x 50ft space in Waterloo Road. With two employees, they produced one £150,000 yacht in the first year. In 1998 they occupied the 35,000 square foot Spitfire Quay at Southampton where the famous fighter was produced during the war, followed by a further 7,000 square feet at Saltmarsh Park, Lymington. In addition to yachts for Whitbread and Volvo round-the-world races, as well as four America Cup contenders, plus luxury vessels, Green Marine has produced twenty-four Mersey, thirty-seven Trent, and forty-two Severn class lifeboats for the RNLI. With over 150 employees, turnover has reached £10 million.

An aerial photograph of Lymington in the late 1920s. The last horizontal row of houses, towards the top left of the picture, are those in Western Road, beyond which are local gardeners' rented allotment plots. Immediately beyond the allotment boundary is Lymington cottage hospital, almost hidden behind a clump of trees. Opened in 1912, following a £600 public appeal as a memorial to King Edward VII, the hospital was built by local firm Stone & St John after fundraising events including musical concerts in the Morant Hall, Brockenhurst. In 1929 a wealthy American visitor, Barkley Henry, and his wife were treated at the hospital, and as a token of his gratitude he presented the hospital with a new operating theatre, X-ray and physiotherapy rooms, although his wife died upon their return to the States.

Stanford Hill rises from the foreground of the photograph, with the imposing three-storey Highfield houses along the centre. Just before the

Chapter 5

AROUND THE TOWN

Stanford Road and Queen Street junction can be seen the original Stanford building works site, complete with clock tower, which became South Coast Garages. A recession in the early 1980s led to the Stanford Road site becoming a Safeway supermarket, and the company finally vacated the town in 1989, leaving Ampress to become an industrial park.

There were several private schools around Lymington by the beginning of the nineteenth century, with a small minority of less fortunate pupils whose fees were met by the Fulford and Anne Burrard charities. It was not until 1834 that Mrs Anne St Barbe, a widow from the well established local business family, generously donated £220 to purchase a half-acre site off New Lane on which to build a school for poor Lymington children. She also defrayed the cost of houses for the schoolmaster and mistress.

Thus the National School was opened on 11 January 1836, built to accommodate 160 boys taught by male teachers, and 120 girls by spinsters, also pupil teachers apprenticed for five years. With children having to pay a penny per week, doubled to two pence in 1879, truancy was a constant problem in Victorian times, exacerbated by pupils having to walk long distances to school in foul weather. Extra classrooms were added in 1879, an Infants' school built on the opposite side of School Lane in 1888, and by 1909 the whole became a Church of England school.

A major reconstitution in 1949 saw senior children transferred to Priestlands School (first housed temporarily at Brockenhurst), then in 1972 the juniors, along with those from the Cannon Lane school, amalgamated at the new County Junior School on sports land off Avenue Road, with the infants following in 1992 to an adjacent new £1.1 million Church of England Aided School (pictured). This left the original St Barbe School vacant until opening as the town's museum in 1995.

This handsome Thornycroft vehicle marked the first local bus service, starting its Lymington-Milford-New Milton service in August 1904. It boasted a 20hp engine and a four-speed and reverse gearbox, and was able to climb the one-in-ten gradient of Lymington Town Hill in second gear. Complete with glass windscreen, and curtains along the sides of the four raised tiers of seating for seventeen passengers, the Thornycroft travelled some sixty miles each day at an average speed of 12 to 15mph, on solid rubber tyres. Though this service proved popular, it was withdrawn at the end of that same summer as such heavy vehicles were prone to become stuck on badly-rutted roads, forcing passengers to alight.

Hants & Dorset Motor Services' omnibuses introduced more comfortable and reliable transport across the New Forest from the early 1920s. Buses from their Lymington depot introduced a regular service to Beaulieu in 1925, which two years later was extended to Hythe, and then Calshot. Some double-decker buses towed fuel-saving producer gas-plant trailers during the Second World War, when petrol was at a premium. Hants & Dorset eventually gave way to Wilts & Dorset.

Until the Turnpike Act of 1755, roads around Lymington had been in a generally terrible state. Pigs routed the gutters, with yokes round their necks to prevent them invading houses. Road repairs were effected by ploughing, before faggots (bundles of twigs bound together) were laid in the deepest ruts, then ploughed over again. The first recorded expenditure in the church books is £2 10s 4d for repairs to town roads in 1685. The Turnpike Act introduced tollhouses with gatekeepers collecting fees at each end of the town: 1½d for a rider on horseback, 4½d horse with cart or carriage, cattle and sheep rated by the score. Although these tolls led to improved roads, they were unpopular with travellers.

BELMORE LANE
LYMINGTON

Belmore Lane, pictured before 27 May 1913. On that fateful day the six thatched cottages seen furthest in this picture, belonging to Mr 'Postman' Brown, were destroyed in the 'Great Fire' at Lymington. The town's firemen attended with their 1897 horse-drawn fire pump, but were unable to prevent the cottages being gutted despite hauling all the thatch off the roofs, leaving the families homeless. The pedestrians are seen walking past the Millwright's Arms,

advertising Strong's Romsey Ales. In 1836 John Hosey had been the landlord there, and in 1851 William Bran was the brewer. The pub's last licence was issued on 7 February 1915. In the distance is the entrance to the expansive Belmore Dairy Farm, its fields long since covered in bricks and mortar.

On the extreme right is the mason's yard, now occupied by Hoare Banks the monumental masons. The Lymington founder, Major Banks, was succeeded by his son David, whose letterheads proudly boasted 'Patronised by Queen Victoria'. The firm provided headstones for the Queen's dogs which died at her Osborne House holiday home, also a 5ft Gothic headstone, paid from her own purse, commemorating sailors and lifeboatmen who drowned in a tragedy off the Isle of Wight. When David Banks emigrated to Canada in the early 1950s the firm became Hoare Banks, acquired by Eric and Ray Hoare whose family firm was founded in London in 1810. It is now continued by Ray's son Stephen, the founder's great-great-great-great-grandson.

A festival was held in Lymington on May 29 1856, celebrating peace with Russia after the Crimean War. An illuminated gas star formed a novel part of the entertainment – alas this was not a success as the gas pipe proved too small. Earlier, on 25 January of that year, the mayor Richard King had approached Lord Panmure with the suggestion that a Russian gun captured in the Crimea might be given to Lymington. Following approval, the town made a subscription for a suitable iron carriage on which the cannon be mounted, manufactured at Woolwich as proposed by the War Office. The cannon was erected in the centre of the road at the northern end of New Street. There it remained until disappearing midway through the Second World War. Its destination remained a mystery until, in 2001, a clue was unearthed in the old photograph album of Tyrrell Stanbridge. Son of a Kent railway signalman, he too joined the South East & Chatham Railway as a thirteen-year-old trainee, before serving with the Northants Regiment in France in 1918. He was later employed at Southampton, where he was commended for organising the D-Day invasion traffic, before becoming the top hat and tails

stationmaster at Charing Cross. He had also been the Lymington Baptists' Sunday school superintendent, and this wartime picture from his album shows the cannon strapped on a flatbed lorry, about to be towed on a barge for Yarmouth. Was the cannon melted down at an Island shipbuilder's foundry for ships' phosphor-bronze fittings?

The greatest change in Lymington town centre traffic management came in 1964. Pictured prior to that time is Priestlands Place, also known as Soapy Lane, an exceedingly narrow street with the Temple Gate across the entrance to prohibit all wheeled access – indeed, young boys caught riding on bicycles were apprehended by the local constabulary, and fined on appearing before the town's magistrates. On one side of the lane was the County Council's Lymington stores depot, with their Civil Defence store opposite. Priestlands Place also accommodated the town's first Labour Exchange, later occupied by Mr G.H.W. Ward's greengrocery and general store. Seen on the left is the substantial Ashdon House, where Mr R. Reid carried out his dentistry practice. On the right is Priestland's Dairy, operated by the Hawkins family for many years, while next door is Miller's the butchers, previously owned by Mr S. Hayward.

All motorised vehicles had proceeded in a two-way traffic flow along Queen Street and Stanford Road until 1964. Priestland's Dairy and Miller's butchers shop were then demolished, along with all properties to the rear along the lane. This enabled a one-way traffic system to be introduced around Stanford Road, Queen Street and the newly-widened Priestlands Place.

At the time this photograph was taken, soon after 1900, the Lymington Quay area, along with Cannon Lane (now Cannon Street), was rarely visited after nightfall, such was the reputation of the ruffian inhabitants. Seen on the extreme left, on the corner with Quay Street, is the Yacht Inn where in 1863 the landlord was Thomas Phillips, and imbibers could relish Mew Langton's Osborne pale ales brewed on the Isle of Wight. It closed on 28 December 1911 and became Langley's confectioner's shop. Next door were the premises of W. Smith, baker and shipping supplier, which later became a faggot and pea shop. Then comes the Ship Inn, whose landlord in 1784 was William Bay. A six-inch board bedded in clay was installed just inside the door to keep out the high tides until this inn was rebuilt in 1936. At the end of the row was the grocery and swap shop run by Mr Greenfield, one of the ferrymen who charged a halfpenny each way when he rowed passengers to the opposite side of the river. The goods train is seen reversing along the railway bridge into the marshalling yard with three railway sidings, along with cattle pens for animals offloaded from the Yarmouth ferries, from where many were driven up Station, Gosport and High Streets to Topp's slaughterhouse at the top of Town Hill.

Today, residents in expensive accommodation around Lymington Quay enjoy more salubrious surroundings. Shops have given way to the inevitable estate agents, and the Ship Inn has, over the years, been extended to the end of the row, complete with open-air riverside tables for customers' drinks and meals.

committee comprising local businessmen, seen in this picture outside their timber and corrugated-iron clubhouse. With a par 35 for the nine holes, Bill Warwick was appointed club pro. and green-keeper, while the licensee of the Chequers Inn, Fred Cole, was also a tutor. In 1937 the course was again flooded as the sea wall was breached during a violent storm. Club president John Akerman of Beaulieu, chairman of Associated Newspapers, who would arrive at the course by chauffeur-driven Rolls-Royce, feared war was imminent and the Golf Club reluctantly closed.

Nowadays this four-mile coastal stretch, from Lymington River to Hurst Spit, is a nature reserve commanding European and national recognition. Since 1973 the County Council has acquired over 500 acres of some of the most unspoilt scenery in southern England, mostly wetland with salt and freshwater lagoons hosting rare creatures. The reserve is popular with walkers and ornithologists, with over 250 different bird species being recorded.

Lymington Golf Club was formed around 1893, with a 12-hole course laid out just inside the sea wall, below sea level. In 1910 this was reduced to 9 holes, and five years later membership reached sixty, the bogey for the course being 82. Many visitors enjoyed this 'good sporting course with plenty of natural hazards', which was forced to close in 1916 after a great tidal wave breached the sea wall in this Oxey Marshes area. Following its reopening in the mid 1920s, membership reached 200 with the

Following the opening of the Southampton-Dorchester railway in 1847, a public meeting was held at Lymington in August 1853, approving a motion 'to adopt measures for securing a branch railway from Brockenhurst to this town.' This led to the formation of a syndicate of local businessmen to promote such a railway, and in 1856 the Town Council approved a Bill, leading to the mayor sending a petition to Parliament. An Act was passed in 1856, with the Railway Company empowered to purchase the quay from Lymington Corporation, and the toll bridge, for £5,000. Construction of the four-mile railway line, with three bridges and two manned crossings, began on 8 January 1857, and was completed the following January, before the line was officially opened on 12 July, to the accompaniment of the Town Band and church bells. A temporary timber station was used until the substantial brick structure was completed on a former marshland site. The Lymington Railway was taken over by the London & SW Railway in 1879, who also acquired rights of the toll bridge. In 1884 the line was extended across the River to the new Lymington Pier station. In 1922 the London & SW Railway gave way to the Southern Railway, which ultimately sold the toll bridge rights to Hampshire County Council, which extinguished traffic and pedestrian tolls in 1968.

Electrification led to the last steam train leaving Lymington on the night of 2 April 1967, packed with some 200 passengers in three carriages and twenty-three riding on the footplate. As this marked driver Bert Farley's retirement after fifty years on the railway, he wasn't too concerned at any prospect of being disciplined.

Union Hill, Lymington.

Union Hill in 1919, since renamed East Hill, with Mrs Flo Pearce and her son George pictured in the foreground. Behind the fence on the right was a large field, opposite the old gasworks. There in a large marquee, to the delight of young and old for miles around, the annual John Sanger's Circus was staged, also Bartlett's Fun Fair every May and October. The arrival of such entertainment was a momentous occasion, with crowds flocking to witness the parade along Lymington streets.

The circus was heralded by a band seated in a wagon drawn by four horses, marking the start of a half-mile procession of more horse-drawn wagons carrying pretty young ladies in spangled tights, followed by, to the astonishment of youngsters, cages bearing such fearsome creatures as lions and tigers, a procession of elephants using their trunk to hold the tail of the one ahead, and clowns and acrobats. James Bartlett established his Fun Fair at Blissford, near Fordingbridge, in 1840. Horses used to haul the wagons gave way in 1889 to showmen's steam engines weighing up to seventeen tons. These took on water from New Forest streams en route to Lymington, with Mr Bartlett insisting on a final polish at the town's boundary. Youngsters eagerly rode on his New Forest Gallopers roundabout, which cost $\frac{1}{2}$d for children, 1d for adults. The Fair continued until the Second World War, when Harry (Farmer Fatty) Golding who weighed over twenty stone, sold his field and it became Fairlea Road council house estate.

Ernest Newman, valet to Col. Charles Vandeleur-Craig at The Orchard, Hordle, married Marie Victorine Moreau, French-born cook to Major James Cillyer-Blunt of Priestlands, in 1914 at Lymington, and together they took over these shops at No. 2 Southampton Road, a confectioner's on the left, and a café on the right. To the rear of the café was the Tea Room where customers were served food, and several local organisations such as Lymington SJAB held their meetings, along with wedding receptions and dances to the accompaniment of local musicians. One regular dancer was Richard Dimbleby, who toured the New Forest area in his little Austin 7 'Bumble Bee' car as a *Southampton Echo* reporter, before going on to become a prominent BBC radio and television presenter. In 1930 Ernie Newman and his wife moved to larger premises, at No. 74 High Street.

Consequently Alf Jennings, who had been working for the bakers Fortts of Bath at their expansive bakery and restaurant at Nos 84-86

High Street, acquired No. 2 Southampton Road in 1930, and converted the two shops into a bakery and confectioners, with one entrance. Alf's son Ron, the only boy amongst seven children, had just completed his education at Lymington Council School in Cannon Lane, and promptly joined his father in the new family business. The old Tea Room remains part of the bakery, still with its original wood floor, roof and wall panelling. Ron is now assisted by the third generation, his sons John and Stephen.

exonerated owing to the ship's incorrect charts. He attained the rank of Rear-Admiral and is buried in St Paul's Cathedral. This picture shows crinolined ladies playing the sedate game of croquet in front of Grove House in 1866, when it was rented for £120 per annum by James Harding for his spinster daughters, Adeline and Margaret. Following his death in 1868 the daughters bought the property for £2,400, the sale including twenty ordinary shares in the Lymington Railway Co.

Utilised as a furniture warehouse during the Second World War, Grove House was acquired by crime and black magic author Dennis Wheatley for £6,400 in 1945. He wrote thirty of his seventy-four books in Lymington, and personally laid over 60,000 bricks on walls around its perimeter, including serpentine curves for extra strength. He placed Grove House up for auction in 1968, along with 1,500 books and 1,000 bottles of spirits, before moving into a London flat. The property was sold for £29,000 to Hoburne Investments Ltd whose MD, John Burry, intended making it his home, until planners retracted earlier refusal by allowing Grove House to be demolished and replaced with eighteen two-storey houses.

George Burrard, a lawyer and one of Lymington's two Members of Parliament in 1685, purchased Rope Walk north of Grove Road from Thomas Bromfield in 1705, where he built Grove House. With the property and grounds substantially enlarged, Grove House was sold in 1809 for £3,500 to Capt. John Bingham, who led a distinguished career during constant actions against the French and Spanish navies. He was reckoned to have received the vast sum of £40,000 prize money by capturing enemy vessels. Court-martialled in 1800 after his vessel, bound for the West Indies, grounded on rocks, he was

Wellworthy had humble beginnings when, just before the First World War, John Howlett took over South Coast Garages. His car repair business was close to bankruptcy when most of his mechanics left to fight for their country, but in 1916 Mr Howlett obtained an order to produce 18lb shells for the Army. The Stanford Road and Vicar's Hill factories produced 35,000 shells before Mr Howlett's determination led to contracts for 10,000 piston rings for Gnome Monosoupape aero engines at 1s 1d apiece, followed by orders for Bentley aero engines and AEC bus engines. Wellworthy was established as a private company in 1919. Thanks to a patented hammering machine, with emphasis on quality and technical improvements, the company, with just over thirty employees, exhibited at the first Motor Show at Olympia in 1922. Continued success meant more machinery was needed to cope with vehicle orders, and Wellworthy was responsible for curing an oiling-up problem with Rolls-Royce aero engines, resulting in the successful Schneider Air Race winner, and ultimately the wartime Spitfire fighter aeroplane.

The new large site at Ampress was opened in 1939, and the two factories worked round the clock in vital war production. By the end of 1945 annual sales reached £1,759,529, with £34,413 profit after tax. More factories followed at Ringwood, Salisbury, Weymouth, Plymouth and Waterford in Ireland. By 1975, 1,800 staff were employed at Lymington alone.

They call it progress. Occupiers of houses in Waterloo Road were left marooned after incessant rains and a double tide resulted in the river banks being breached in the great flood of October 1909. These rowers brought relief supplies along the length of this road, whilst just to the south, Bath Road properties were hit ever worse, with water rising halfway up the staircases.

Advance ninety years. By now the Environment Agency has given assurances that the newly-constructed sea wall, extending from the Keyhaven-Pennington marshes, round the toll bridge road and along the eastern side of the river, would in all probability preclude further flooding. But on Christmas Eve 1999, torrential rains saw water pouring from the opposite direction off the New Forest, unable to escape into the sea owing to the new sea-defence wall, and again flooding Waterloo Road houses up to a depth of four feet! Waterlogged Richard Baker (pictured) from No. 26 commented: 'I've lived here since 1953, and this is the third time I've been flooded indoors – the last was in 1989, two weeks before Christmas.' Once again steps were taken in a bid to prevent a similar occurrence.

ymington became infamous for its smuggling activities, dealing in such commodities as lks and brandy, invariably centred round its any inns, particularly the Quay area where ontraband was hidden in drainage tunnels. This 930 picture shows the cobbled Quay Hill, where 1607 town mayor Luke Stevens died of the lague in his house. Seen at the foot of the hill is he Solent Inn, dating back to around 1700, riginally an impressive gentleman's residence omplete with bowling green to the rear. By 843 the landlord was George Stevens, and soon fter the turn of that century Mr Yateman was censee, who weighed about twenty-three stone, erified when he travelled by train for a football natch at Brockenhurst, where several men laced him on the station scales. Until 1880 The olent brewed its own beer, passing on to Mew angton who closed it in February 1939, everting to a private residence.

At the foot of the hill, on its junction to the ght with Quay Street, was The Alarm, named after Mr Weld's famous yacht – some of the vessel's timbers were even used for the Baptist church pews. One Quay Hill pub still surviving is the King's Head on the right, where the landlord in 1836 was Thomas Avery. Other occupants on the hill were Mrs Fanny Walden's general store, hairdresser 'Lukie' Frampton, 'Soldier' Webb's sweet shop, and Mr Winkworth who bought rabbit skins. Nowadays Quay Hill businesses are rather more upmarket, including the inevitable estate agency.

on his wife Harriet's demise that, in 1877, he built the Sunday school to the right of this picture for Woodside children as a memorial, complete with small belfry. He lived in the nearby thatched Delawarr House.

The school premises was also used for other weekday activities, such as boxing, where Woodside lads were instructed by a nun, Sister Martin, who would herself glove up to demonstrate the rudiments of attack and defence. Young men also formed the near-invincible Woodside Wonders football team, who played on the paddock behind, using the Sunday school as their changing room. With National School headmaster Billy Taylor amongst their players, when matches ended they washed in the adjacent brook – though against advice one lad used water in a cattle trough, and died of cholera. The cup-winning Woodside Wonders were still competing after the First World War, but the Sunday school has long since been converted into a private residence, though the little belfry remains, minus bell.

Such was the esteem in which Lymingtonians held Admiral Sir Harry Burrard Neale, owner of the Walhampton estate who provided all the iron columns for street lamps around the town, that upon his death in 1840 they erected the Walhampton Monument, a 76ft granite obelisk on the eastern side of the river, with most of the £1,482 3s cost being raised by public subscription. In 1892 Francis Crozier, owner of the monument site, presented the freehold to the Lymington Corporation together with £100 for future maintenance. Such was Mr Crozier's grief

Deeds for the thatched Wagon & Horses Inn, alongside the eastern side of the Lymington River, date back to 1643. Originally known as the Wagon Ale House, it was reputed to act as the stopping place for wagoners waiting for the ebb tide to cross the ford, in days before the dam toll bridge was built illegally by Captain Cross in 1731. Country folk also left their donkeys and carts there whilst crossing to Lymington in the halfpenny rowing ferries for their weekly shopping in the town, the donkeys being tied up for 1d, or 3d if stabled. Mr Elgar was the landlord in 1800, and the inn was rebuilt in 1908.

This photograph was taken in 1894, the year after an unfortunate shooting tragedy at the inn. There was much intrigue across the country at that time concerning the infamous Ardlamont Shooting Case, in which the case hinged on whether Lieutenant Hamborough could possibly have shot himself from behind. Thirty-eight-year-old gamekeeper Henry Card, of Snooke's Farm,

employed by Mr J.P. Heseltine of Walhampton House, got into conversation with London visitor John Bligh at the Wagon & Horses, insisting such a shooting feat was indeed feasible. To demonstrate, he raised his double-barrelled shotgun, believing it to be empty, and pointed the muzzle to his head from the rear. Alas, Card proved his point to the extreme, for the gun was loaded and on pressing the trigger died in the tap-room from mortal wounds.

Lymington Poor House was built in 1738 to shelter the homeless, poor and vagrants in return for work, at a cost of £248 10s 2d, on land adjacent to the site of the mediaeval tithe barn. Richard Budden was appointed the first Master at an annual salary of £10, whilst Henry Hackman provided necessary medicines and appropriate surgery. The parish overseer drew up a list of sixty-four suitable for apprenticeship, comprising males between the ages of seven and twenty-four, and females from seven to twenty-one or marriage. A total of 141 children were indentured between 1700 and 1773. The Borough authorities threatened a fine of 40s if the Workhouse dung-hole was not cleansed and trenched, as the effluent was considered a nuisance to passers-by. Such were spending restrictions that in 1760 the 1s 6d weekly payment for the food of every inmate was reduced to 1s 3d, the funding being levied principally through a Poor Rate on property owners. It was agreed in 1780 that if an inmate was seen walking the streets not wearing the identification letters LP, the Master's pay would be taken off for the week.

A meeting was held in 1788 with parish representatives from Beaulieu, Boldre, Brockenhurst and Lymington with a view to building one common Workhouse, to form a Union. The Lymington representative voted against, and it was forty-eight years before such Workhouse was built on the Poor House site for £4,500 to accommodate 270 inmates, surrounded by three acres to grow vegetables. Later renamed Lymington Infirmary, it was converted in the 1930s into two in-patient wards on the ground floor, with a maternity ward above, the latter facility being discontinued soon after the Second World War. In 2002 the local Health Authority sanctioned the closure of the Infirmary, deemed unfit, in favour of multi-disciplinary visiting teams in conjunction with Social Services.

When King Charles II ordered a royal survey of his property and tenants around the New Forest in 1670, Sir James Worsley, Bt., laid claim to Pilewell and ninety acres of land, at an annual rent of 6s 2d. Subsequent ownership by the Arundell and Senior families led to Thomas Weld, of Lulworth Castle, purchasing Pylewell House and its 1,950 acres down to the Solent shoreline for £45,000 in 1801, for the benefit of his second son Joseph, a keen sailor. He added wings on either side of the house, maintaining a lavish lifestyle. An original member of the Royal Yacht Squadron and a skilful designer, Joseph began constructing yachts on Pylewell Hard, until instructing Thomas Inman to build the 85-ton cutter *The Arrow* at his yard on the Lymington River. Joseph went on to spend £30,000 on this and two successive boats, the 127-ton *Lulworth* and 193-ton *Alarm*, all dominating prestigious yacht races. Next he ordered the *Alarm* to be sliced in two and lengthened into a 248-ton schooner, one of the few English boats to defeat the celebrated *America* in the America's Cup.

In 1850 Joseph sold the Pylewell estate to George Peacocke for £43,700, and four years later it was purchased by William Williams-Freeman for £47,835. By 1874 William Ingham Whitaker had acquired the mansion and 1,400 acres for £72,000, after inheriting Marsala wine estates in Sicily. He was succeeded by his son and grandson, both named William, both playing significant roles within the Lymington community. The grandson died a bachelor in 1988, when the estate passed to a nephew, former Coldstream Guards officer Lord Teynham, who took up residence with his wife Elizabeth and their ten children. At one time the estate employed 150 staff, but in 1951 the east and west wings were demolished as an economy measure.

Sir Giles Rooke, Kt, Judge of the Common Pleas, settled in Lymington and married Harriet, sister of Sir Harry Burrard Neale and a lady of great beauty, having modelled for Sir Joshua Reynolds who was a frequent visitor to Lymington. Sir Giles left five sons: Giles, William, Harry, George and Leonard, all born in the town. William bought the expansive Woodside property in 1830, one year before he died. His son William Wowen Rooke, an officer with the 2nd Life Guards, died at Woodside on 8 April 1804, and a marble drinking fountain was erected in his memory, originally sited at the western end of St Thomas' Street, now on the Bath Road recreation ground. He was survived by two bachelor sons, Colonel Henry Rooke born at Woodside in 1842, and Captain Algernon Wowen Rooke of the 84th Regiment. Col. Rooke opened his seven acres of landscaped Woodside Gardens one Sunday a month, when around 300 people would enjoy this tranquil setting to the accompaniment of Lymington Town Band. In the mid-1920s he munificently bequeathed Woodside House and its gardens to Lymington Corporation.

Ten years later an idea was mooted to convert the Victorian house into a museum, a serious omission in the town. The Council's deplorable inaction resulted in this house falling into disrepair and being vandalised, necessitating demolition. In 1985 the idea of a museum was resuscitated by retired director Ted Marsh who formed an enthusiastic steering committee. As he ignored obstructions and doubters, the long-held dream became a reality 1995 with the opening of St Barbe Museum in the old Church of England School off New Street, with 12,000 items given or loaned covering Lymington, New Milton, Milford, Hordle, Sway and Boldre, dating back to Stone Age flints.

ymington folk have always subscribed generously towards their hospital. In 1913 his original cottage hospital was built as a emorial to King Edward VII after fundraising y the 5,000 residents realised £800, on land onated by the lord of the manor, Keppel ulteney. Accommodation comprised male and male four-bedded wards, single-bed emergency ard, operating theatre, X-ray room, dispensary d kitchen. In addition the matron, Miss D. ynch, retained her sitting room on the ground oor, and one for the other nurse, her sister Miss Lynch, on the first floor. As the number of tients rose to 800, a further £2,200 was raised 1928 to extend the wards and add one for ildren, whilst personal funds provided a private rd block. Later, local residents took part in a ompetition to purchase two plots of land on hich a nurses' home was constructed for £2,500. During the Second World War two mporary' prefabricated wards were added, for tients who included wounded soldiers and

prisoners-of-war from the Setley camp. Another public appeal was launched in 1980 for £150,000 to add a new casualty unit and pathology lab; eventually an amazing £450,000 was raised before the official opening three years later by Princess Anne. By 2002 the deteriorating 'temporary' wards were still in constant use, as the Health Authority, after two failed attempts, made a third application for a new hospital under the Private Finance Initiative scheme, having already paid £1.5 million for a covenanted site at Ampress.

Nine generations of the Burrard family lived at Walhampton from 1668 for the next 215 years, representing Lymington at Parliament between 1679 and 1835. Elizabeth Burrard, widow of Thomas, had bought the sixty acres in 1668 for £1,060, and the central block is the house of 1711 built by Paul Burrard II, whose eldest son, Harry, added two wings around the time he was created a baronet in 1769. The photograph was probably taken between 1870 and 1880. John Heseltine purchased the property in 1883 from William Mount, who foreclosed the mortgage on the estate which had been raised when Sir Harry Paul Burrard succeeded in 1871. In 1936, on the death of Lady St Cyres (née Morrison), the estate was placed in the hands of trustees John Morrison and Leslie Watts on behalf of Charles Morrison (born 1932), who succeeded in October 1953. When the trustees sold Walhampton House and 86 acres in 1948, Dorothy Brewer and the Revd Philip Hayllar paid £10,000 outright, and the £20,000 balance was the mortgage with the Morrisons. The pair started a school with twenty boys, and in 1954 the estate was purchased by joint headmasters John Bradfield and Peter Lawford – but for them the school would have closed as Charles Morrison threatened to call in the mortgage in 1960. The Earl and Countess of Wessex opened a performing arts centre for the 360 pupils in 2002, Walhampton School having amalgamated with Hordle Cliff House School, Milford, five years earlier.

ymington River was once navigable as far as Ampress, then considerably wider and deeper owing to the strong double tides. Such a situation changed dramatically in 1731 when an unauthorised dam was built across the River by William Cross of Boldre, a Merchant Captain related to Robert Pamplin, to whom Charles I had granted 'in consideration of a great debt and faithful service done' all mudflats between Hurst Castle and Calshot. The dam, 500ft long, 30ft wide and 20ft deep, affected navigation and enraged the mayor and burgesses, who ordered the town clerk to devise a proper case of trespass against the Captain 'for digging and carrying away the land at Bridge Green, which was then in possession of the Corporation.' Capt. Cross died before the proceedings commenced at Winchester Assizes in 1739, when Charles Colbourne – a portly man fond of bull-baiting and carousing – was retained by the council. He lost the action against widow Cross to demolish the causeway, leading to even greater indignity as she and tailor William Lyne exacted tolls on all who passed across the dam. In 1899 the future

King Edward VII, on one of his first car rides, passenger of the second Lord Montagu, was decidedly amused when forced to wait for a considerable time by gatekeeper Mr G. Gooden, venting his fury after a driver had sped across without paying.

This 1907 picture shows a horse and cart passing through the toll gate, the driver having paid his penny fee, whilst a lady pedestrian passes her halfpenny to the toll keeper in his office. In the foreground is the Freemasons' Arms, offering cider, ginger beer, lemonade and lime juice all at 2d per glass. It was not until 1958, after the toll bridge had passed from the Railway to the County Council, that tolls were finally lifted.

As the Armed Forces massed along the coastline in preparation for the D-Day invasion of France, Lymington Airfield was one of four temporary advanced landing grounds laid in the area, on farmland a mile east of the ferry terminal. The 1,600 yard east-west and 1,400 yard north-south runways, surrounded by blister hangars, were constructed in 1943. In April 1944, 50th Fighter Group of the 9th US Army Air Force arrived by train, their convoy ships having berthed at Liverpool the previous day. With their P47 Thunderbolt fighters flown in by ferry pilots, the airmen lived in tents around the airfield, soon fraternising with local young ladies The 10th, 81st and 313th Fighter Squadrons underwent intensive air training in readiness, with one pilot, Capt. 'Bull' Nelson (pictured), killed in a Bobcat crash. On 1 May 1944, these squadrons were engaged in the first fighter sweep over Caen, followed by dive-bombing missions during the invasion, until they finally departed on 25 June for bases in France. The Lymington airfield returned to farmland, though the American millionaire Charles Burnett III of Newtown Park still retains a private air strip and an original blister hangar.

Twelve makeshift airfields around the New Forest played similar vital roles. In addition to RAF and US pilots there were Canadian, Free French, Polish, Australian and Czech personnel, with over 4,000 stationed at one time at nearby Beaulieu Heath. In August 2002, before a crowd of 1,000 with a Red Arrows fly-past, a memorial surmounted by a Dakota propeller was unveiled at Holmsley to commemorate those aircrews and local civilians who served on these wartime Forest airfields.

Lymington parish church, dedicated to St Thomas the Apostle, dates back to around 1250, though there is evidence that a chapel existed long before that time. A mortuary chapel was added in the north-east corner by the Courtenays around 1325, where members of that family are buried under a large grey slab. There was merely one monthly service for several years, with the parish clerk performing burials. The first known incumbent was William Ekerden in 1396, and at one time the curate was Henry Francis Lyte, author of the hymn *Abide with Me*. During the civil wars the church was gutted whilst occupied by Puritan soldiers, and by 1660 was in a sad state. Townsfolk set to work, and in 1670 the south transept was demolished to be replaced by the present tower, with a clock added in 1674 and a peal of six bells in 1684. Since 1756 the church has been enlarged many times, and in 1911 there was much restoration, thanks to the £1,000 legacy of Mrs Martha Earley.

Chapter 6

LOCAL CHURCHES

The churchyard extended to the centre of the High Street until 1821, when Sir Harry Burrard Neale presented the churchwardens with a $\frac{1}{2}$-acre plot to the north for a cemetery, thereby allowing the street to be widened as the old burial ground was cut back.

A Magdalen chapel once existed in Pennington, mentioned in 1276, and up to 1839 the parish was ecclesiastically and civilly part of Milford. The original St Mark's church was then built, consecrated by the Bishop of Winchester, along with some adjoining land as a burial ground. Complete with spirelet and bell and seating 200 including the gallery, the church boasted a barrel-organ which emitted two tunes, the 'Old Hundredth' and the National Anthem, other musical arrangements being performed by parochial instrumentalists. One early preacher, the well-known author Canon Kingsley, was so impressed with the cleanliness of Mrs Miller's cottage that he presented her with the substantial sum of half-a-crown. A parsonage was built in 1846 on land donated by lord of the manor, John Pulteney, whose widow, Elizabeth Evelyn, later acted as benefactor for the new Upper School, which opened in 1852.

Church services were held in that school whilst the present St Mark's church was under construction, to be consecrated by the Bishop in 1858 – an occasion of great rejoicing by a large congregation. Laid out in the form of a Latin cross partly on the site of the previous church, from which the original bell was salvaged, it holds nearly 400 people and cost £2,038, realised from voluntary contributions and Church Building Societies. To mark the cessation of the Boer War in 1902, one worshipper donated £10 to start an organ fund, leading to the acquisition of such an instrument four years later for the sum of £300, plus £38 10s for its electric motor. The churchyard was enlarged in 1904, and in 1927 the Revd A. Crick dedicated this handsome lych gate in memory of his wife Fanny.

ymington Baptists were hardy folk. As dissenters during the time of Cromwell, they met secretly in each other's homes for fear of arrest, and carried out baptism by total immersion in Hatchett Pond, Beaulieu, at all times of the year, earning the soubriquet 'Dippers'. They moved to their present site in 1769.

In 1791 there was dissension in the church, resulting in a second place of worship being set up temporarily at the ironmonger's shop on the corner of New Street, now Boots, with William Mursell as preacher. By 1834 the original building was inadequate, so using the old materials, the present church was erected for £1,625, with legacies amounting to £1,275, so merely £350 was left to be raised. The building included a day-school for 140 scholars in the rooms beneath, used as a British Restaurant in the Second World War.

Lymington Baptists had their own 125-strong Band of Hope (seen here marching past an Angel Hotel horse-drawn coach in 1911), a

Boys' Brigade with its own band, Girls' Brigade, and other adult and youth organisations. In 1978 large areas of dry rot were eradicated after a gift-day realised £1,600, with members carrying out much of the work themselves.

The roots of Lymington United Reformed Church date back at least to 1672, though earlier worshippers met in small private-house groups. As Presbyterians, they congregated at the Old Town chapel, Nos 31-32 St Thomas' Street (pictured), and the first recorded minister was the Revd Robert Tutchin, who arrived in 1672 after being ejected from the curacy at Brockenhurst. In 1821 the gifted young Revd David Everard began twenty years as incumbent, publishing musical and religious works. He composed the anthem *Hark the Trumpet* and secreted the town trumpeter, old Macey, under the pulpit – who at the appropriate moment let forth a loud blast which left elderly members of the congregation suffering from palpitations; the deacons insisted this was not to be repeated.

Their name changed to Congregationalists, and by 1842 numbers had swelled so that larger premises were sought. Nearby Quadrille Court was purchased, but before development commenced there was an exchange transaction for the present site in the High Street. Contract for the new church and hall was accorded to Reeks & Rickman, the cost, along with the adjoining parsonage, being £4,500. The first service in the New Independent Chapel, seating 180, was held on 28 October 1847. The title changed to United Reformed in 1972. Ambitious plans were drawn up in 2003 to include a central entrance instead of doors on each side, and demolish the old hall and caretaker's cottage to be replaced by a single-storey extension, at a cost approaching £1 million.

It was not until 1829, after the penal statutes were repealed, that Roman Catholics became totally emancipated. In 1800 a Jesuit Mission was established in Lymington by a French émigré priest, who attended his countrymen taken prisoner during the wars and those who sought refuge in this port at the time of the French Revolution. A chapel was opened at Pylewell House on the eastern side of the river, belonging to the Weld family, who also owned Lulworth Castle in Dorset. They paid for the land at the foot of Town Hill on which Lymington Catholic Church was built in 1859 to the design of Mr Hansom (of horse-drawn hackney carriage fame), with the school (pictured) added alongside in 1860. There were just two classrooms, with Pylewell estate children amongst the original pupils.

By 2002 there were 118 pupils on the school roll, with head teacher Mrs Irene Cradick leading five teachers and ten support staff.

Following a twenty-year battle, the construction of a new £1¼ million Catholic school finally commenced in that year on a site compulsorily purchased off Ramley Road, Pennington. The parish priest, Don Clements, dug the first sod and told pupils this was the first time he had used a spade in earnest since shovelling sixteen tons of coal each day as a fireman on the footplate of main line steam railway engines.

This picture was taken in October 1931, when St Thomas' sacristy was about to be rebuilt. From left to right are churchwardens Edward Hapgood, of No. 19 High Street and Richard Bower (the church choir stalls were donated in his memory), and the vicar, the Revd Montague Bethune, who had the habit of riding his bicycle with a raised umbrella in one hand during wet weather.

Back in 1907 the parish had bought and adapted Blenheim House, renamed Church House, at No. 56 High Street. That property was sold in 1926 with the proceeds, supplemented by subscriptions, enabling the construction of the Parish Hall, complete with stage, for more secular use, at the end of Emsworth Road. Plans announced in 1979 by the vicar, Jack Haselden, to sell the Parish Hall in order to erect a new church hall on the site of 112 graves to the immediate north of St Thomas' caused so much indignation, particularly from the watchdog Lymington Society, that a three-day consistory court was convened in the Parish Hall. The judge, Prof. Arthur Phillips, as Chancellor of the Diocese, heard pleas from both sides before approving the plans. The Parish Hall and half-acre site was sold by Jackman & Masters for £201,000 at public auction, and the new church hall erected to the design of eminent local architect Roger Pinckney, who had been involved in rebuilding war-damaged Liverpool Cathedral. The new hall was dedicated in 1981 by the Bishop of Southampton, John Cavell, before a congregation of 350. Amongst those present was the Revd Howard Bostock (Lymington vicar 1947-74), whose father Charles had also been the incumbent from 1906 to 1922.

Few can have contributed more towards Lymington's commercial success than John Howlett. In 1897 he signed indentures for 4s a week as a fourteen-year-old apprentice mechanic with the renowned steam engine manufacturer Charles Burrell & Son in Thetford, Norfolk, where his father worked as a carpenter. Leaving in 1904, John tried several jobs before joining Daimler the car makers at Coventry. He then moved to Wolseley, where he worked on Queen Alexandra's car, before joining Austin.

In 1912 he successfully applied for the vacancy of manager at South Coast Garages in Lymington. John's determination saved the company and after the First World War it became known as Wellworthy.

He was elected to Lymington Council in 1921 and became mayor in 1930; he was eager to promote harmony when, two years later, Lymington Borough's boundaries were controversially enlarged to incorporate the councils of New Milton, Milford, Hordle, Pennington and part of Sway. Determined Lymington be spared the earlier unemployment

Chapter 7

PERSONALITIES AND INSTITUTIONS

he had seen in Sheffield, his two factories in the town operated twenty-four hours of shift-work during the Second World War, and by 1975 employed 1,800 in the town. Made an OBE, John retired in 1957 and concentrated on farming. He died in 1977.

A ncient Lymington courts were conscious of the dangers of fire. Presentments on 4 May 1727 decreed 'we present that Moses Rawkins take down or otherwise secure from fire his working shop by the 4th of June next on pain of Twenty shillings'; and 'we present that the Chimney in Mrs Rigg's Brewhouse [is] very much out of repair and very dangerous as to fire and that the same be sufficiently repaired and secured by the 11th Instant on pain of Twenty shillings.' In 1919 the Council replaced their 1897 hand-pump with a second-hand horse-drawn Shand Mason steam fire engine purchased from Bournemouth Corporation, which had first acquired this machine around 1900. Capable of providing two fire-fighting jets at 100psi within five minutes of turnout, it consumed 28lb of steam coal per hour. The Borough of Lymington Fire Brigade had its own strict rules, to comprise fifteen men or more selected by the Council, with one unpaid drill per month, with a 6d fine for absence, or dismissal if missing for two drills or two fires in a year. Remuneration for attending a fire was 2s 6d for the first hour and 1s per hour thereafter, with commandeered bystanders paid 6d an hour. The alarm bell was rung atop the large water tower near the Sports Ground, summoning the firemen and their two horses stabled in the Angel yard.

In 1928 the Council purchased its first motorised fire engine, housed in Southampton Road by the water tower. Lymington's Auxiliary Fire Service performed courageously during the Second World War blitz on Southampton. The firemen moved into their new station by the Town Hall in 1969.

The changing face of agriculture. Hay in the bottom picture has been cut by a horse-drawn mower with cutter-bar, then left to dry, before being turned by a horse-drawn rake, next manually pitch-forked on to a hay-cart, thence drawn by horse for the farm labourers to build a haystack, again lifting the hay with their pitchforks. By contrast, the modern picture shows now a single tractor towing a Reco round-baler at Sadlers Farm, Pennington, able to discharge thirty-five 4ft 6in hay bales covering three acres within an hour, employs just one man.

Joseph William Smith, born in Tolpuddle, Dorset, in 1851 (seventeen years after six Dorset farm workers were sentenced to transportation for seven years for administering an unlawful oath to form a trade union in that village) arrived in Lymington to purchase Sadlers Farm in Lower Pennington Lane, as well as the Chequers Inn. Joseph, who had two sons, Walter and William, and a daughter Evelyn, continued farming until the day he died in 1936. By the

time Walter's son Eric had joined his forebears, the family had also acquired South Sway Farm, Warborne Farm in Boldre, and Lower Buckland Farm, from where the main dairy delivered milk around much of the Lymingon area. Eric's son Richard took over Sadlers Farm in 1959, and bought the adjacent Woodside and Ridegway Farms. After suffering a stroke in 1997, his sons Simon and Daniel have become the fifth generation of farming Smiths on this land.

War with such tasks as collecting sphagnum moss, used for surgical dressings. Miss Tod became scoutmistress for sixteen years, and in 1924 eight scouts attended the world jamboree in Copenhagen. This picture shows the troop immediately prior to the Second World War. Tragedy struck in 1948 when the hall, with its wood-panelled interior walls, was destroyed by fire, along with equipment. A new site was purchased off Marsh Lane the following year. The troop continues to thrive under Brian Stone, who joined as a Cub in 1946, becoming scoutmaster in 1961. Merger talks with Pennington Scouts were effected in 2003.

The 9th Lymington Sea Scouts were formed in 1921 by Robert Hole. Their first meeting was held in Newman's Rooms, and later in a stable block to the rear of Heathcote House in St Thomas' Street. The boys learned elementary seamanship in two dinghies on the river, also camping, hiking and sports. In 1926 they attended the international Sea Scout jamboree in Antwerp. The present headquarters were opened by the Duke of Kent in 1991.

The 1st Lymington Scout troop is amongst the oldest in the country. In 1908, the same year Sir Robert Baden-Powell inaugurated the Scout movement, a few Lymington boys were formed into a Scout troop by Francis Patmore. They shared facilities with the Cadet Corps in the Drill Hall, until a commodious corrugated-iron hall was erected in Emsworth Road. Mr Patmore remained scoutmaster until appointed county secretary around 1912. The Lymington scouts played their part during the First World

By the time St Thomas' church tower was erected in 1670 – though there could have been a central tower earlier – bell-ringing was becoming more scientific and organised, so the Lymington ringers escaped the evil reputation for drunkenness, godlessness and noise earned by their sixteenth-century predecessors. As a Puritan place, loyal to the House of Hanover, the Lymington bells were rung at Coronations and public events, and in 1715 to commemorate success over the rebels at Preston. The cost of their bell-ringing appears to be included in the Mayor's accounts. Huge crowds gathered, to the accompaniment of Lymington Band, when a new octave of church bells arrived on horse-drawn carts in 1901, the tenor weighing over a ton. The bells were received by the vicar, Canon Benjamin Maturin, and hung on a new steel frame. A quarter-peal was rung in 1904, and a

three-hour peal two years later. The ringers are pictured on an annual outing to the Isle of Wight in 1913.

Nine of the bell-ringers resigned in 1929 after the vicar criticised them for not staying behind for services. Today's bell-ringers are much more responsible, marking the centenary of the bells in 2001 under their captain Rex Corke (above, third left) and still ringing for Sunday's two services.

found himself on the little 4,850 ton tramp ship *Ramsay* bound for Argentina, in charge of its sole 12-pounder gun. At 11 p.m. on the night of 27 April 1918, Norman spotted a 100ft vessel with rigged masts travelling faster than the *Ramsay*, despite no wind. His suspicion that this was a German U-boat in disguise was well founded, and after the *Ramsay* had avoided a torpedo, Norman fired around twenty-five rounds from his gun, blowing off the conning tower and setting the sinking submarine on fire. The Argentinians hailed Norman a hero, but on his return the Navy was not unduly impressed, calling him out of the ranks on a routine parade to be presented with a cardboard box by the duty officer, inside which he found his DSM.

After the Second World War, he joined the newly-created DHSS and was transferred in 1953 to Lymington, where he married Methodist church secretary Miss Edna Starks. At the Queen's Golden Jubilee celebrations in 2002, the mayor, Jean Vernon-Jackson, and her predecessor, Pauline Elsworth, are seen presenting commemorative mugs to Norman and seven-year-old Michael Down, one of all Lymington and Pennington schoolchildren to receive this award. Norman died in December 2002.

Son of a Nottingham Methodist minister whose church was bombed in the First World War by a Zeppelin, Norman Gooderidge celebrated his 104th birthday at Lymington on 13 August 2002, eighty-four years after being awarded the Distinguished Service Medal. Such was his poor eyesight that he wore spectacles from the age of six, but managed to volunteer for First World War service with the Royal Navy by peeping between his fingers during an eyesight test. After serving on the cruiser HMS *Drake*, he

One of a Basingstoke builder's eleven children, Herbert Goodall (inset) won an engineering scholarship to Hartley's University, Southampton. In 1910 he rented around seventy acres of Lady St Cyres' Walhampton estate at Lymington as a dairy farm, later acquiring further land from nearby Elmer's Court and Walhampton estates, building up his Bampton's Farm to 150 acres. He served on the Southampton Co-op development committee for twenty years, was Lymington Community Centre's original vice-president, a New Forest Rural and Boldre Parish councillor, and governor at South Baddesley and Brockenhurst Grammar schools. Changing his political beliefs from Tory to Socialist, Herbert delivered speeches standing on a box in Lymington High Street. Between 1933 and 1939 he hosted up to 300 Southampton schoolchildren camping free on one of his fields, and organised rallies there for Young Socialists, including future Chancellor of the Exchequer Hugh Gaitskell (centre) and future Speaker of the Commons Dr Horace King (right), seen taking part in an egg and spoon race!

In the mid-1930s Herbert's brother Harry, a builder, bought the farm. Following Herbert's death in 1976 aged ninety-three, the farm was made over to his son Alan, who also served on New Forest and Boldre councils, and was elected Hampshire chairman of the NFU. With the farm producing fifty tons of strawberries annually for major supermarkets and the London market, Alan's son Brian became the third generation at Bampton's, whilst his daughter Margaret is Kent NFU chairman.

With farm incomes diminishing, Brian and Pennington business consultant Rick Tapson won a planning appeal to transform a low yield area of Bampton's Farm into a nine-hole 'pay and play' golf course in 2002. Pictured left to right: Alan Goodall, Rick Tapson, Brian Goodall.

horses, which eventually gave way to a 6hp Fowler steam traction engine owned by U. Cowie, seen above en route to Liphook in 1909. Ford's later hired the Wallis & Steevens steam traction engine belonging to Len Lance, who ran his own scrapyard and removals business on the low-lying peninsula between Lymington railway station and the river. Len's steam engine was commandeered for First World War service, towing military equipment in convoys on Salisbury Plain, and such was the superior speed of his engine that the military added an extra water carrier behind – but wily Len remained the fastest by furtively draining all the water!

Ford's steam engines were superseded by mechanised transport when this massive Leyland lorry, with open driver's cab, was acquired to haul the removals trailers, pictured outside Ford's High Street premises, now the Pine Shop. The Leyland gave way to large modern integrated furniture lorries. 'Mac' Matthias worked as Ford's removals driver for forty years, pictured on the left with Mr Church, a porter.

After Charles Ford and his wife Emma opened their furniture shop at Nos 47-48 St Thomas' Street, residing over the premises with the cottages known as Church Hatch to the rear, their daughter Sarah joined the family business, and later Alfred Isted upon their marriage. It was at this time that the company added furniture removals to its business credentials, firstly with large trailers drawn by

Admiring Lymington lads walk alongside the young Lymington Cadets as they march, headed by their own band, along the High Street on their way to the Army's tented camp in the forest, off the northern boundary of Sway. Escort is given by the town's police sergeant on his bike as they pass, on the extreme left, the Old Bank House which once housed the local St Barbe & Co. Bank (later acquired by Lloyd's) before it was converted into an hotel and café during the 1930s. The Army Cadets, along with the town's Hampshire Volunteers Territorials, met in the Bath Road drill hall, originally built as a sail loft for the shipyard on the opposite side of the road. No. 99 High Street acted as the Volunteers' armoury and accommodation for their drill instructor. There were rifle butts on the marshes inside the sea wall, with a small brick building to store ammunition. Close by, along with the golf course, were asparagus beds, this produce being sent by rail from Brockenhurst to London.

Today's local Army Cadet Force unit (below) still trains twice weekly in the Drill Hall. In 2001, led by Colour-Sgt Ian Wilson, they captured the prized New Forest Shield after competing against seven other detachments in a rigorous three-day competition at the Lee-on-Solent training camp.

LYMINGTON CADETS MARCHING TO SWAY. MAY 19 1905

Captain Harry Doe with his wife, pictured outside their Broad Lane home on the occasion of their golden wedding in 1915. He had served before the mast on square riggers before being made skipper of the 98ft steam-powered *Mayflower*, which had been introduced on the Lymington-Yarmouth ferry route in 1866 two years after her construction at Newcastle. A well as joining her sister ships *Solent* and *Red Lion* on daily cross-Solent passages, and towing half-barges introduced in 1836 to carry livestock the *Mayflower* also ventured east on trips to Portsmouth, and there were moonlight evening cruises past the Needles to the accompaniment of Lymington Town Band. Captain Doe went on to take command of the 120ft *Lymington* following her launch at Southampton in 1893, representing a considerable advance with her compound oscillating surface condensing engines.

Captain Doe died around 1930, with the entire family, including great-grandson Albert, made to stand around his deathbed to witness hi final throes. The Captain's son, Harry jnr was a steward on the *Mayflower* and *Lymington*, while grandson Tom Doe joined the Southern Railway's cross-Channel ferries out of Southampton at the age of fourteen, later serving at Lymington on the *Freshwater*, *Lymington* and *Farringford*, until retiring as the terminal's marine foreman at the age of sixty-five. Two great-grandsons, Ken and Alby, signed indentures as Berthon Boatyard apprentices on the Lymington riverfront, where Alby remained for sixty-two years, while Ken became a carpenter on the *Queen Mary* and Union Castle liners. Capt. Doe's great-great-great-grandson James Doe (pictured) passed out in 2002 as a Sub-Lieutenant on the destroyer HMS *Edinburgh*.

ymington Band, pictured on the occasion of their silver jubilee in 1933, has been in continuous existence despite two world wars. On January 1883, twelve musicians met at the Angelsea Temperance Hotel to consider forming a band, receiving material support from the hotel proprietor, Mr W. Batt. Their first practice was in Hardey's Dairy, Buckland, later in a room at the Sea Water Baths, then in a small hall at Woodside, before settling at the Literary Institute, where the band continues to practice to this day. The original bandsmen were all abstainers, and frequently played for the Cornwallis-Wests at Newlands Manor in front of the Prince of Wales (later King Edward VII), who was highly amused by the title Lymington Temperance Band!

Besides playing at regattas, society dances, parades and carnivals – including the annual Lymington confetti battle romps – such was their high standard that for the first eighty years of its existence they were never out of the prize lists at festivals, thanks mostly to tuition from Mr A. Muddiman, a doyen of band trainers. They did lose a few important players when the local factory Wellworthy Band was formed towards the end of the Second World War. After half a

dozen title changes over the years, Lymington Military Concert Band performed a centenary gala night concert at the Masonic Hall. Nowadays, under conductor Doreen Pullen, Lymington Town Band maintains its fine tradition.

In 1936 twelve fishermen held a meeting at the Rising Sun Inn, New Milton (pictured, built in 1903), to form Lymington & District Fishing Club. Their numbers grew, but were forced to live a nomadic life as the committee met in various pubs and clubs around the Borough, including the Anchor & Hope and Londesborough hotels in Lymington High Street. In 1996 a Building Fund was launched with the aim of acquiring their own headquarters, starting with £8 14s 6d in the kitty. Moves to acquire a prefabricated former school building came to nothing due to financial and planning reasons.

In desperation, Club members cheekily entered a planning application to erect a building on the New Forest District Council's own land off Bath Road – and unbelievably were told 'Yes'! The euphoria diminished when the Council offered to split the land into three, for the Yacht Club, Sailing Club and leaving a boggy shrub-covered area for the Fishing Club. The generous offer of an adjoining 200ft x 75ft plot came from Mrs Nausicaa Pinckney, whose architect husband Roger had been instrumental in rebuilding part of Liverpool Cathedral demolished by the wartime blitz. Club members fundraising included jumble sales, dances, bingo and waste-paper collection, so that a handsome 48ft x 20ft headquarters complete with bar and weighing-in room was finally opened in 1993, the £70,000 cost being offset by £21,000 grants, and members' £20,000 interest-free loans. With over 200 members, including national representatives and a vibrant junior section, this Fishing Club remains one of the largest in Hampshire.

Yacht building has been carried out along the Lymington River for centuries, but Dan Bran has become something of a legend – constructing dinghies by eye, drawing their contours on the dirt floor of his large wooden shed (pictured) by the sea water swimming baths. Born at Woodside, he was named Daniel Plat Bran by his mother, after local Parliamentary candidate Colonel Platoff. Unable to read or write, Dan signed indentures for a seven-year apprenticeship at Edwin Inman's Lymington Shipyard (now the Berthon), which stipulated he should not enter matrimony, fornicate, play cards or dice, nor haunt taverns and playhouses, starting at 2s a week and eventually reaching 14s. He worked as a spar maker at Poole before opening his own business in the riverfront shed in 1910, designing the first 11ft *Lymington Pram* in 1911, followed by the *Lymington Scow*, still raced today.

Of unkempt appearance and sometimes irascible nature, he hunted on the marshes with his 12-bore shotgun. When his repeated warnings to the Southern Railway were ignored, concerning the wash from their speeding paddle steamers damaging his moored dinghies, he demonstrated by firing both barrels of his shotgun

into the *Solent*'s canvas-covered wheelhouse. Dan and his wife lived in Coastguard Cottage, next to the Mayflower Hotel, where he was a benefactor until he died in 1950. Later his dilapidated shed, deemed by some to spoil the view across the Solent, was destroyed by a mystery fire one Sunday afternoon.

(plumber), mariner, butler, shoemaker and gamekeeper. The ladies marching along the High Street (pictured) formed the Elizabeth Chinery Lodge. After moving to the Foresters' Hall in Ashley Lane, which had earlier housed some of the town's earliest schools, the Foresters' Arms became the Hearts of Oak. Members' next hired the Literary Institute, before finally settling at the Royal British Legion Club.

One of the founder-members was Lymington brewer William Knight (born 1830), successively followed by his cabinet-maker son John, grandson William – a tailor in the town – then great-grand-daughter Margaret Knight, covering an entire 150 years. William devoted his life to this cause, assisting members to make provision for times of sickness and distress, and acted as treasurer for some sixty years until his death at the age of ninety-four, whilst his young daughter used an antiquated typewriter to address membership cards. In September 2002 the Foresters donated a public seat in Bath Road to mark their 150 years, as well as the twenty-two years' secretarial service of the late Eric Bye.

At a meeting of the Foresters' Friendly Society high court conference at Westminster, London, in 1851, approval was given to open a Court Yelverton in Lymington. Original meetings were held in the Blacksmith's Arms in Southampton Road, which became known as the Foresters' Arms in 1859. Original members' occupations included blacksmith, coachman, servant, yeoman, whitesmith

For over twenty-five years Williams Banks operated as builder, estate agent and undertaker at No. 77 High Street, forbidding his apprentices to enter into matrimony, play cards or dice, or haunt taverns playhouses. In 1859 J. Rashley and J. Springer acquired these premises, with an extensive yard to the ar, and became one of the most prestigious builders in the area, with contracts including the imposing ctoria Hotel on Milford cliff top. In 1905 Tom Rashley took on his son Percy, Frank Totterdell and chard Bower (indentured 1905) as partners, paying their labourers 7d an hour, plasterers and plumbers d. With 110 employees, annual staff outings were by way of two hired Royal Blue coaches (max. speed mph); one is pictured below with Richard Bower standing second left, Percy Rashley third left, and anager Alf Northover, seated far left.

Other prestigious contracts included the town's Lyric Cinema in 1913 (now Waitrose), the ternationally-renowned Chewton Glen Hotel at New Milton, and restoring St Thomas' church. ank Totterdell died in 1938, Percy Rashley in '39, and Richard Bower in '42, whose son Ted retired om the business in 1954. Later directors included Mike Matthews, Gordon Burgess, Arthur Trigell and ary Cornwall who, faced with 'an intolerable rent hike' by a development company at the end of its ase in 2001, vacated No. 77 High Street after 142 years to relocate in Pennington with Rashley's eight maining employees.

By the time Robert Hole was ten months old, both his parents had died. He was brought up by a Lymington aunt, Miss Herringham, and following First World War service became a teacher at Radley and Stowe. Giving up this career in 1933 to concentrate on social work, he called a public meeting in the Parish Hall thirteen years later, attended by 260 people, with the idea of forming a Community Association. This was realised on May 13, with subs of 2s 6d. Classes were held in hired rooms or members' homes, and in 1947 a $\frac{3}{4}$-acre site was purchased off New Street for £1,500. Mr Hole bought four ex-RAF hutments at his own expense, and on 2 November 1948 Mayor T.B. Gibson opened the first section of the Lymington Community Centre project, with membership reaching 550. The first warden, Matilda Fitch, received an annual salary of £200, and lunches were cooked on the premises. Another of Mr Hole's ambitions, a public library for the town, was achieved in 1949 when the County Council added this facility in the Centre's grounds on a 99-year lease at £1 per annum with no rent review – until a new library was opened in Nort Close in 2002.

A cinema has existed at the Centre almost since inception, and expansion has led to a veritable honeypot of activities, ranging from classes in dancing, art, woodwork and upholster to yoga, computers and navigation. By the jubile year of 1996 there were 2,433 members, 111 affiliated organisations, and eighty-six weekly classes. With around 10,000 people passing through its doors each week, the Centre is held a model of its kind, at home and abroad.

Born in China, son of a Methodist missionary, Basil Fletcher-Jones' family lost all their possessions there during the Boxer Rebellion and were forced to flee to the United Kingdom. Basil went up to Oxford before completing his studies at Salisbury Theological College. Following his ordination in 1940 he became curate at St Thomas' church, Lymington, first under the stern Revd 'Monty' Bethune, and later the more genial Revd Kenneth Lamplugh. Striking up an immediate rapport with younger members of the congregation, to whom he was affectionately known as 'Tink', Basil formed the Church Youth Club and the 10th Lymington Church Scouts, who met in a small hut behind the Parish Hall. He is seen in this photograph with the original Youth Club members, who enjoyed keep-fit sessions, ballroom and country dancing classes, amateur dramatics, and raised a football team which competed on the Sports Ground on Sunday afternoons – provided they had attended church that morning. Three original couples later married.

After six years in Lymington, 'Tink' sailed for Australia at the invitation of the Bishop of Perth, where he became youth leader, cathedral curate and college chaplain. He returned in 1954, and following eight years as ordination candidates' committee secretary at Church House, Westminster, spent eighteen fulfilling years as Rector at Walton-on the-Hill, Liverpool. Upon retirement in 1980, he served as honorary curate at Brighton before his death in 1984. Still fondly remembered by his old Lymington Youth Club and Scouters, they held a reunion in September 2002 at Woodside Park (pictured), planting a commemorative ornamental birch tree as a lasting memorial.

On 28 July 1902, the Lymington Nursing Division of the St John Ambulance Brigade was formed by Mrs Elizabeth Chinery, seen seated in the centre of the top picture with her original nursing volunteers. Earlier, a St John Association had been formed in the town to provide first-aid training, along with men in their ambulance division, which fell by the wayside until resurrected for the 1914-18 war. The two divisions operated separately, with female and male members not allowed to attend lectures together or carry out first-aid practice in the same room. Mrs Chinery, whose husband Edward was mayor from 1909-11, took great pride in her uniformed nurses and won many prizes. They tended wounded New Zealand troops at converted hospitals in Lymington and Brockenhurst during the First World War.

By 1921 St John's regular meeting place was the tea room behind Ernie Newman's café in Queen Street; in 1927 they moved to the British Legion clubroom; then three years later rented the Girl Guides' hut behind the Lyric Cinema. Besides attending public events, the division operated the town's ambulance, first a Sunbeam before fundraising paid for a new 1931 Standard. Assistance was given at the hospital in the Second World War, and after 78 years' existence they obtained their own headquarters in New Street – until ejected by the Health Authority in 1999. Premises were acquired in Ashley Lane, until December 2002 when they took possession of their own £750,000 headquarters on the Gordleton industrial estate, shared with Hampshire Ambulance Authority as the Brigade's tenants.